Management
in a Quality
Environment

Also available from ASQC Quality Press

Implementing Quality with a Customer Focus
David N. Griffiths

Reengineering the Organization: A Step-by-Step Approach to Corporate Revitalization
Jeffrey N. Lowenthal

Excellence Is a Habit: How to Avoid Quality Burnout
Thomas J. Barry

The Service/Quality Solution: Using Service Management to Gain Competitive Advantage
David A. Collier

The Change Agents' Handbook: A Survival Guide for Quality Improvement Champions
David W. Hutton

The ASQC Total Quality Management Series

TQM: Leadership for the Quality Transformation
Richard S. Johnson

TQM: Management Processes for Quality Operations
Richard S. Johnson

TQM: The Mechanics of Quality Processes
Richard S. Johnson and Lawrence E. Kazense

TQM: Quality Training Practices
Richard S. Johnson

To receive a complimentary catalog of publications, call 800-248-1946.

Management
in a Quality
Environment

David N. Griffiths

ASQC Quality Press
Milwaukee, Wisconsin

Management in a Quality Environment
David N. Griffiths

Library of Congress Cataloging-in-Publication Data

Griffiths, David N., 1935–
    Management in quality environment / David N. Griffiths
        p.   cm.
    Includes bibliographical references and index.
    ISBN 0-87389-222-4 (alk. paper)
    1. Total quality management.   2. Leadership.   3. Customer service.
I. Title.
HD62.15.G75   1994
658.5'62—dc20   94-3470
                                                            CIP

10 9 8 7 6 5 4 3 2 1

ISBN 0-87389-222-4

Project Editor: Kelley Cardinal
Production Editor: Annette Wall
Marketing Administrator: Mark Olson
Set in Avant Garde and Janson Text by Linda J. Shepherd
Cover design by Daryl Poulin
Printed and bound by BookCrafters, Inc.

ASQC Mission: To facilitate continuous improvement and increase customer satisfaction by identifying, communicating, and promoting the use of quality principles, concepts, and technologies; and thereby be recognized throughout the world as the leading authority on, and champion for, quality.

For a free copy of the ASQC Quality Press Publications Catalog, including ASQC membership information, call 800-248-1946.

Printed in the United States of America

 Printed on acid-free recycled paper

 ASQC
Quality Press
611 East Wisconsin Avenue
Milwaukee, Wisconsin 53202

To Barbette, Michael, and Megan
for their continuing love and support.

Contents

Foreword ix
Preface xi
Acknowledgments.. xvii

Part I: The Quality Environment

Chapter 1   Beware of Disguises...................................... 3

Chapter 2   A Quality Environment Is Customer
Focused.. 11

Chapter 3   A Quality Environment Uses a Customer
Satisfaction Methodology 21

Chapter 4   In a Quality Environment There Is
Commitment and Discipline............................ 35

Chapter 5   In a Quality Environment There Is Teamwork 41

Chapter 6   The Quality Environment Evolves Over Time 47

Chapter 7   The Quality Environment Requires a
New Type of Management............................. 55

Part II: Management (in a Quality Environment)

Chapter 8   Seeing Management as a System...................... 65

Chapter 9   Create and Maintain a Quality Environment
(Culture)... 71

Chapter 10 Management and Support of the Quality Process ... 81

Chapter 11 Coordinate and Facilitate the Planning and
Resource Allocation Process 89

Chapter 12 Develop and Implement Policy 99

Chapter 13 Coordinate and Facilitate the Customer Satisfaction
and Improvement Pursuit 109

Chapter 14 Teach/Coach/Mentor/Develop......................... 115

Chapter 15 Management in a Quality Environment 123

Part III: Processes of a Quality Environment

Chapter 16 The Planning and Resource Allocation Process...... 131

Chapter 17 The Performance Plan and Review Process 143

Chapter 18 The Compensation System 153

Chapter 19 Quality Policies and Practices......................... 161

Chapter 20 The Line of Sight Process 167

Chapter 21 Management in a Quality Environment
(Summary).. 173

Appendix A 177
Appendix B 181
Suggested Reading 187
Index 189

Foreword

A fundamental change is slowly but surely overtaking American business. The change is about the way we manage and a significant modification in the way we think and act as managers. This change has been given many labels, but "management in a quality environment" fairly describes the thrust. The focus in this new environment is on customer satisfaction, both externally and internally, and a commitment to continuously improve all that we do in our business.

This change only occurs when management wills such a change, and therefore, there is not a uniform wave of change sweeping across all business. Rather the change occurs as a significant event, company by company, as leaders gain understanding and demonstrate leadership for change. The nature of this process results in the side-by-side existence of companies with extremes in management style. This will continue for an extended period of time (probably decades) until one day we will look back unable to believe that the standard business practice was once a management of power, control, top-down communication and tell-do processes.

One of the trailblazing companies managing in a quality environment is Citizens Gas and Coke Utility of Indianapolis. The leadership team at Citizens Gas has created an extraordinary change with gratifying, measurable improvement of the business. Citizens Gas President and CEO, Don Lindemann, has been a hands-on leader of the change process, and Dave Griffiths has been the team leader who assumed the full-time task of education and implementation. As CEO of a large company attempting a similar course of action, and as a member of the Board of Directors of Citizens Gas, I have followed the change implementation with great interest. I believe Don and Dave to be exceptional leaders making a significant contribution to their company and their community as they pioneer a better way to manage.

It is my belief that an individual who accepts the responsibility of running a company now has two levels of responsibility. The first is to operate the company within the established system to achieve the objectives of the company. The second is to improve the system used to run the company. The second is significantly the more difficult task and demands great knowledge, courage, and leadership. A good leader addresses both issues.

In this book Dave tells us why we need to change, compares traditional management ways to better ones, and shares knowledge that is only gained through experience. This book will be most helpful to the leader who seeks to improve the management system.

ROBERT M. CLARK
Retired General Manager
Allison Transmission Division
General Motors Corporation
Indianapolis, Indiana

Preface

I have been in management for over 35 years, from line foreman to senior executive, in a very large corporation as well as in a very small, in for-profit and not-for-profit corporations, in manufacturing, in services, and even in government. Someone with my experience would be apt to claim that so much has been learned from these many years and their variety that this book is warranted. The truth is, however, that this recounting is based on what I've learned in recent years, years that have been the most enlightening and rewarding of my work experience.

This book is about management in a quality environment and is based on experience gained from being leader of the quality implementation team at Citizens Gas and Coke Utility in Indianapolis, Indiana, and from those as a member of the executive support team, made up of our CEO and his staff. It is about sharing lessons learned (and still being learned) as a member of executive management in an environment pursuing quality. It is a comparison of management lessons learned recently to those of previous practice. Finally, it includes reflections made from numerous observations of management in other than quality environments.

One of the challenges faced in implementing quality is that management styles, techniques, systems, and processes are of an often unchallenged traditional mode developed over years and years of management theory dating back to the late 1800s and early 1900s. Then the issues were those of mass production and uniformity, when control of everything, including the human resource, was essential. Today it is time to reexamine, to redesign, and to rethink previously unquestioned "truths." It is also imperative that we not repackage old ways in the name of quality.

Although scholars like W. Edwards Deming and J. M. Juran have preached for years we should change our ways, too few of us have listened. Perhaps it is because too few of us have been students of management while functioning as managers. Usually, we begin our managerial endeavors expected to fill the shoes of the one before us, who had also filled the shoes of the one before. Consequently, management evolved with little change to practice or conduct, continuing to concentrate primarily on performing functional tasks consistent with long-standing policies and procedures. Time was never found to think anew, to improve, to reengineer our managerial activities and their processes and systems.

Management in a Quality Environment is more than a sequel to my first book, *Implementing Quality with a Customer Focus* (ASQC Quality Press, 1991). The latter is a how-to-implement endeavor tracing more than three years of initial hands-on experience. This book summarizes key elements from the first book but goes well beyond and adds another four years of personal involvement and observation in the building of a quality environment. This is primarily a what-to-do book. It emphasizes differences between traditional managerial concepts and techniques and those required to lead, manage, and support the quality culture successfully.

This work includes a brief explanation of the quality process methodology and its customer focus. Customers are described as being internal as well as external, and the quality process shows how to satisfy and eventually exceed customer expectations through continual improvement. This process begins with assessing customer requirements, and then ensuring that the delivery system produces the required (desired) customer-identified need. The process is completed by measuring and monitoring the resultant product, service, or output to identify improvement opportunities. It is in this third and final phase that the organization's quality pursuit begins to add value to its output, product, and/or service, to in fact exceed the basic expectations of the customer. This process and how it is implemented is detailed in *Implementing Quality with a Customer Focus.*

In *Management in a Quality Environment* there is a greater emphasis on management, not only in the collective, organizational sense but also as applicable to the individual and always with a customer focus. In the book I share my own experiences over several years as I evolved from one managerial style to one quite different. Perhaps the reader, too, will begin to appreciate how managers should aspire to go beyond mere functional competency to greater cross-functional organizational worth. In this expanded view of managerial responsibility, emphasis is placed not only on the traditionally known tasks but also on those necessary to support the progress of the organization and to lead it. Management in a quality environment requires skills of the individual well beyond those used in customary directive (bossing) situations. It requires of us an ability to determine whether leadership, management, or support is the appropriate skill to use. It requires an ability to shift from one to the other or to mix, and definitely to balance. The old style of management is easy to do compared to the challenges of leadership, management, and support. Those who develop the broader capability will have tremendous organizational worth and an individual competitive edge. This book is intended to assist in your development of this broader capability by making you more aware of the differences in managerial styles and techniques, and in starting you toward an understanding that managerial activities are interrelated and should be thought of as processes influencing the system producing goods or services.

I begin by discussing a quality environment in my own terms. I use my own terms because I'm alarmed at the many (*too* many) organizations that state they have begun quality efforts that are only new words disguising old ways. These organizations haven't learned and don't understand what the quality pursuit is about. Instead they see it too often in shallow terms of productivity improvement or cost reduction to increase profits. There are also organizations that direct the quality effort toward activities to improve quality assurance or increase employee involvement. Even these organizations miss the vast potential attainable with the more enlightened approach focused on satisfying customer needs using a methodology understood by all.

Part I of this book shows how to establish a foundation of understanding what a quality environment should be. I discuss the elements management must ensure are provided: customer focus, understandable and usable methodology, commitment to the effort, disciplined adherence to quality concepts and techniques, ongoing education and training, meaningful communication and information sharing, encouragement of organization-wide involvement, recognition of teams and individuals, and a never-ending desire to improve and to be the best. Part I also stresses the importance of leadership, with emphasis on the personal involvement of the organization's top management—either leading, managing, or supporting, but always participating.

Part II shows how to build on the leadership previously established. I discuss how we must see our roles, rethink the vital elements of management, and redefine the key components of the management system. It is my intent to show how we limit our capabilities with traditional functional, task-oriented, and hierarchical organizational practices, while all around us is opportunity beyond expectation. I describe an organization where quality is not separate from the rest of the organization but is everything the organization is about. There are functional and cross-functional opportunities for improvement, and individual and team opportunities where managerial involvement and responsibility exceed simply directing traditional tasks. One's role as manager is more than performing functional activities well; it is ultimately measured by one's effectiveness within the larger system and by the organization-wide impact of one's activities.

Part II also expands the vision of the organization to one of many processes making up a total system of interrelated functions—each dependent on the others—with only one basic purpose: to meet the needs of the customer. Of significant importance to fulfilling this purpose is the environment we create and maintain in which the human resource can flourish.

Examples from a successful management endeavor in pursuit of a quality environment are given in Part III. I describe how the customer focus and its methodology have caused an organization (my own) to evolve to dramatically new ways of doing fundamental organizational activities. In Part III we look at the processes of planning, budgeting, human resource utilization, and managing the organization. I'll also share pursuits in progress, needs not yet satisfied to further demonstrate that the quality journey never ends. A basic truth for management in a quality environment is that there is always a better way to improve the system we lead, manage, and support. One's progress is always evolutionary, from one state to the next. Management in a quality environment is always changing, always improving. It is dynamic.

Acknowledgments

There are so many who have directly or indirectly contributed to this book that I hesitate to begin listing for fear of missing someone. Regardless, I'll proceed with good intentions.

As in my first book, I again express appreciation for the customer focus concepts and methodology learned so long ago from Xerox Corporation, but still so applicable today. Ernst & Young also deserves recognition for its facilitation in the early years of our journey and its continuing assistance. Don Lindemann, CEO of Citizens Gas and Coke Utility, as leader of the executive support team, has been the guiding influence toward most of what this book is about. The executive support team has been a significant source of information and inspiration; therefore I thank my peers, Jim Chenoweth, Jeff Clancy, Marty Dusel, Fred Lekse, Carey Lykins, and Jean Richcreek.

Special mention is deserved for Pam Butcher, director of quality, who worked with Towers-Perrin to design the performance plan and review process so valuable to our quality pursuit.

A few special words are required also for the employees of Citizens Gas and Coke Utility who, in formal and informal teams as well as through individual efforts, are achieving results once thought unattainable. They make management in a quality environment worth writing about.

Part I:
The Quality Environment

1 Beware of Disguises

Don't repackage old ways in the name of quality.

Heed the warning of this chapter's title. I have observed an alarming number of organizations that claim to pursue quality, but that are, in fact, doing nothing new. They continue to pursue improvement (and there is certainly nothing wrong with that) using traditional approaches, approaches based on management concepts dating back to the late 1800s. These organizations often repackage old beliefs about getting the job done and focusing on quality improvement. They believe they have modernized their thinking and ways; they believe they are applying techniques proved so successful by the Japanese and by some U.S. companies.

This error in ways is compounded by we of management, who for a variety of reasons ranging from ignorance to blatant disregard of the truth, continue to practice our craft(?) as we were taught in business school, in our early apprenticeships, and by our personal successes in climbing the corporate ladder. Management, however, is not solely to misguided unsusptecting blame. Some consultants have misguided unsuspecting companies and their need for operational and organizational improvement. These consultants offer only parts of a total quality effort in whatever term or concept management will buy, thus prostituting the opportunity and its potential.

Time and again over the years I've been reminded of how blissful it was for those of us who became early students of quality implementation, how uncomplicated and how basic the pursuit appeared. We accepted with little question that quality is a process, not a program or a project; that it has a beginning but no ending; that it is the concept of continually trying to improve to satisfy customer needs, to exceed customer expectations, and to add value to product and service without adding costs; that the improvement is of the right thing and the right way the first time; and that all of this required a new type of management, leadership, and support, creating a new work environment.

Those successful in the early efforts didn't decide to launch the journey, then delegate the implementation to others; they didn't boss the effort rather than lead it. It was, admittedly, a rather frightening thought to realize the length and breadth of the topic, to acknowledge that the next quarter or the one following might not show the results demanded by those of us in management taught to cost justify everything. Yet now, with many successfully implemented quality efforts to learn from, there is still far too much misunderstanding. Perhaps from this basic truth there is in itself the opportunity to learn, to discover that one's own conventional wisdom cannot direct the approach to quality implementation.

To illustrate more specifically the misdirected pursuits I see most often, let me share those most commonly found. Heading the list is cost reduction, now usually described as productivity improvement. I believe wholeheartedly in the desired outcome of and the need for such projects, but it is the way we go about them that must be reconsidered.

Partial enlightenment can be a dangerous thing. For example, some organizations attempt to achieve productivity improvement by empowering employees to address management-selected improvement issues or to institute self-directed work teams that select issues and develop recommendations. Employee empowerment can be a powerful improvement tool, but it must be properly focused and supported. The focus should be dictated by customer needs and/or expectations, which consequently identify the delivery processes to be considered for improvement. In addition, the improvement effort requires management's attention and involvement, but in ways different than many of us understand, ways that sometimes lead, other times manage, but always support the pursuit. Subsequent chapters will expand on these requirements.

It is, however, pertinent to our discussion here to understand a basic element of a true quality effort. Improvement endeavors have their greatest potential when they are understood and accepted by everyone. Again I'm speaking of the way we in management cause (direct) things to be done. In this case the real issue is establishing and conveying why improvement is to be done and to whom the improvement is important. In order to properly convey this seemingly simple rationale for improvement, management must improve itself and its methods. As managers, we must first be certain we understand why, and when we communicate the rationale, it will be seen as having the same importance by others in the organization. This is more than buy-in. Acceptance, based on understanding and agreement by those most directly involved, must be achieved. Improvement should not be a one-way, I-win-you-lose pursuit. It should have as part of its charter the intent to have everyone win: management, employees, and especially the customer.

I once thought everyone could readily see the obvious need for and logic in the improvement effort, but I failed to understand that the way I see things is not the way they are necessarily seen by others, especially when it comes to productivity improvement. The reason was quite simple. In my organization (and I expect in many others) productivity improvement always meant loss of jobs for some. Is it any wonder that improvement was feared? What we had done traditionally was create winners (those being management and shareholders) and losers (the employees fearing job loss). Today we cannot afford such division. Today our organizations must have a common vision and purpose to survive. We must be together in what we do and what we try to achieve. Collaboration and teamwork cannot become improvement tools in an environment where only a handful benefit. The days of master and slave, of boss and subordinate are gone, but with their demise so too must we rid ourselves of their ways of managing.

This, of course, is exactly what this book is about, new ways of managing organizational pursuits, ways to compound successes, to maximize the effort. Examples of optimizing concepts and techniques come later. For now, it is important to illustrate further the error of a repackaging mentality. The proper focus for improvement pursuits must be established to make them understandable and acceptable to everyone in the organization. If they are not, a well-intentioned endeavor may fail or at least may not achieve results desired or needed.

There are other pursuits in addition to cost improvement or productivity improvement that are also being done in the name of quality. Again let me stress that these and the others that will be listed are not wrong to pursue. It is simply the manner in which they are attempted where many stumble. Traditionally, improvement efforts are segmented or modualized. They are approached as programs or projects having limited focus rather than as a continuous process of improvement encompassing the entire listing of organizational pursuits (see Figure 1.1).

Problem solving is an organizational activity that from the moment of its initiation the effort is focused on negatives rather than positives. The logic of the need for problem solving often gets lost in the perception that something is wrong or broken and must be corrected or fixed. With this often comes a feeling that there must be someone to blame. When this occurs, management has created an environment in which the people doing the work sense there will be a loser. This type of an environment seriously affects people's ability to achieve what might have been accomplished with a different focus and rationale.

Process improvement is another modern-day effort that is only partially successful because it is hindered in its potential through

```
Productivity improvement
Cost reduction
Results improvement
Problem solving
Process improvement
Employee empowerment
Team building
Customer satisfaction
```

Figure 1.1. Organizational pursuits.

inadequacies of managerial approach and attitude. These often stem from organizations traditionally being defined and structured by task or function. The greater opportunity, however, lies beyond the functional boundary where organizations can strive for system-wide, cross-functional, multidepartment process improvement. We have not been taught to think or approach organizational activities this way, and, consequently, this is seen as putting at risk "my" department or area; that is, my turf. In these situations managers as well as their employees fear loss (of importance, of influence, of budget, of salary or wages, of jobs). Working in a quality environment can greatly diminish these concerns, but creating such a culture cannot be simply ordered to be done. Past teachings and experiences limit us, because creating a quality environment takes time; it requires evolutionary changes. Unfortunately, traditional quarter-to-quarter outlook restricts and, in some cases, makes impossible evolution.

A results-driven focus is still another restriction organizations face, especially those with the limited vision or time horizon just mentioned. The repackaging of old ways in the name of quality in these instances takes on an almost all-of-the-above aura. One distinctive feature it entails, however, is the use of measurements and the targeting of dollar or other numeric achievement objectives. In case you haven't already guessed, this is the once acclaimed management-by-objectives approach, or MBO. (Is it any wonder employees look at the managerial ranks with bewilderment and probably amusement? Can you imagine how many different pursuits a long-term employee experiences and suffers through? Is it any wonder the grapevine bemoans program-of-the-month managerial ineptness?) It is not, however, inconsistent to expect positive results from quality implementation, although to be achieved the organization must overcome many historical obstacles. The difference between the old ways and those of quality is focus, and when the focus is on meeting and exceeding customer needs and expectations, positive results will be the consequence.

One of the most potentially damaging but well-intended improvement initiatives is employee involvement, also called employee empowerment or self-directed work teams. Before initiating, we simply must understand what management's role and responsibility must be to achieve success. Organizations place future managers at risk by creating justly founded employee expectations that will not be realized. Instead, in too many instances, the failures of management will be more clearly seen than ever before because of the misinterpretation of what quality is about and what management should do for successful implementation.

Even among those organizations where so much has been accomplished, examples can be found of eroded or limited success because things are still being done the old way. Most often these limitations are evidenced by functional organization structures created to do quality with hierarchies in and of themselves developed as separate departments outside the regular organization. Established in this manner it is no wonder they become bureaucracies unto themselves and/or wither on the vine of opportunity. It is also no wonder they are easily attacked or dismantled. The environment in which successful quality implementation has or is occurring is one where management understands that the endeavor is a routine part of everyone's job, not something someone else provides.

The environment in which teamwork is common and collaboration is the rule not the exception cannot be disguised. It either exists or it doesn't. This is also true about the organization that is focused on customer satisfaction. These two ingredients contain the elements that differentiate between the common organization and the unique, the traditional organization and the quality organization. Management that understands the importance and the power of these will accomplish much more than can even be imagined.

I have in this chapter described several things that the quality environment is not, contrasted with some of what it should be. In the chapters that follow I'll expand on the differences between the traditional organization and the quality organization, differences that don't occur by accident or chance, differences that are created by enlightened management. Before proceeding, however, there remains one last pertinent point.

I don't know who first penned or stated the phrase total quality management, or TQM, but let's reflect for a moment on these words. Of particular significance is the word *total*, with its meanings of "the entirety" and "the sum of all parts." As we discuss in greater detail quality and management, please keep in mind the concept of totality. This chapter provides ample illustration of how quality pursuits too often are only partially attempted. The challenge for today's manager and for those of the future is to envelop all such organizational endeavors into a single, all-encompassing, truly total effort. This effort is completely dependent on management's correct grasp of quality concepts and practices. It is an effort affecting every aspect of the organization, an effort requiring management's comprehension of what its roles and responsibilities are.

2 A Quality Environment Is Customer Focused

Don't focus on pursuits having limited appeal.

Chapter 1 illustrated that there are many choices, programs, projects, or pursuits (perhaps all are better described as temptations) on which an organization may focus. The problem with all such management-driven efforts is that they lack universal, organization-wide appeal, or buy-in, as we now like to describe it. This chapter will show that a true total quality environment can have only one focus: customer satisfaction. All improvement activity should stem from this simple fact.

In *Implementing Quality with a Customer Focus*, I quoted B. Joseph White, Ph.D., now the dean of business administration at the University of Michigan, who stressed, "First, focus upon the customer. The purpose of all work and all improvement effort is to better serve the customer." Later, he completes the rationale by stating, "Quality is a goal people rally around, unlike other operational goals like cost reduction or productivity improvement. Quality opens people up to change because the change is for a good reason. It connects them with the customer and taps the motive of pride in their work."[1]

The issue of focus and its importance seem to be appropriately stated in what Dr. White has provided, but unfortunately managers don't always do well with a "new" thought, straightforward though it may be. Perhaps it is through personal translation that managers bend or alter the meanings and intent. It is imperative, therefore, that managers ensure that there is a common definition of the basic words and phrases used in communicating what they hope to accomplish and why.

Quality, as Dr. White and I use it, means satisfying customers' needs and expectations. It is this focus that is in fact "the purpose of all work." Yet too many of us don't understand and, consequently, neither do our people. Worse yet, this lack of understanding leaves the organization with varied interpretations as to what it is we are about and why. In a quality environment, however, the pursuit is with universal constancy of purpose and disciplined consistency to the customer satisfaction focus. It is worth repeating: The focus of a quality environment must be to satisfy the needs and expectations of our customers. Within this seemingly simple and obvious basic premise all other organizational needs and desires will be addressed: making a profit, ensuring quality products or services, improving productivity, beating the competition, responding to change, employee involvement, or whatever else may come to mind.

Another critical definition is required here. Just as one is apt to translate quality too narrowly, so too may we translate customer. I believe the single most powerful revelation in my quality learning has been that customers are not only external, but they are internal as well. When one begins to think of other departments, of fellow employees, and of subordinates as customers, monumental positive changes occur in the way work is done or, in quality terms, in the way we deliver our outputs, services, or products.

It is important that I immediately emphasize that satisfying the needs and expectations of the external customer must always be paramount. As we strive to better meet the needs of internal customers, we must guard against diminishing external customer satisfaction. The challenge is for us to see our efforts as a total system designed to satisfy our traditional customers. Figure 2.1 depicts the total quality system, driven by customer needs and expectations with all individuals, departments, and suppliers in pursuit of the organization's mission, vision, and goals while sharing the same values. The pursuit, the focus, is toward but one end, to meet (or better yet, exceed) customer needs and expectations. It is this oneness of purpose and understanding that links all

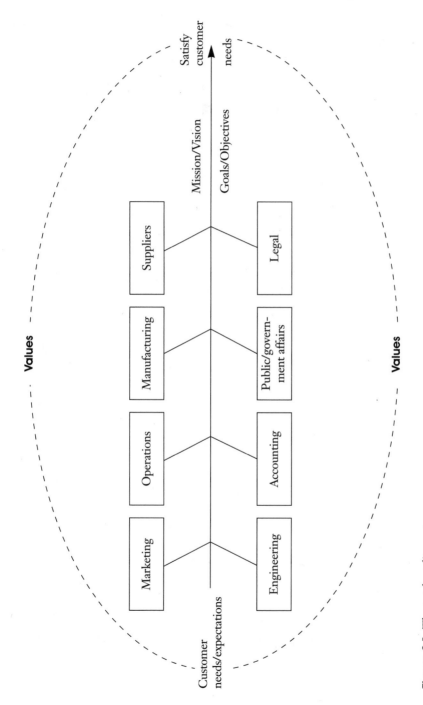

Figure 2.1. The total quality system.

activities and processes toward a single end that, when initiated, is a total quality effort and, when achieved, makes the total quality environment.

It is this linkage that provides the powerful revelation opportunity referred to a moment ago. The focus on internal customers and satisfying their needs and expectations toward improving external customer satisfaction has the potential of transforming the organization from one of departmental boundaries and barriers into one of complementing rather than competing activities. In this new environment information ceases to be hoarded as a power cache and is shared not only within the department but with other departments as well. Collaboration is common, competition is not; partnerships are sought, teamwork prevails; and continual improvement of the system is the goal.

The customer focus when supported by this single-system attitude requires a new generation of management that is long past due. The traditional hierarchical, functional organization restricts not only management but all within it. The organization that is capable of multidepartment, cross-functional teamwork on a routine daily basis is one where processes are seen as related parts of the single system. People working in such an environment better understand not only the organization's mission and vision, but their own role and purpose toward its accomplishment. Consequently, people are better able to fulfill their tasks and to improve on them.

What we are discussing here is the culture of the organization, the environment in which work is done. More than any other responsibility of management, the culture it creates, supports, or maintains (whichever the case may be) is critical to the ability of the organization to provide the desired products and services. Yet, too often, management gives precious little thought or effort to the cultural tasks required to create and maintain the environment. Usually when management's attention is on aspects of the work environment, it is in response to problems or conditions occurring because of management negligence. In other words, involvement is reactive rather than proactive. The recognition of internal customers, however, forces management to address how best to satisfy the needs of direct reports, work associates, and other departments (always within the context of being better able to satisfy or exceed the needs and expectations of external customers).

Some may think consideration of culture is a "soft" issue, but it is far from it. In many ways it is most of what this book is about. Within cultural issues are the keys to unlock many process improvement opportunities and with them the ability to provide ever better products and/or services. This can happen as a result of employees striving to improve their individual and departmental outputs, and recognizing that these are not independent products but are parts of a larger whole. With this recognition comes the capability for multidepartment, cross-functional analysis of how we do what we do. Again, such attitudes and actions are dependent on the way managers conduct the affairs of the organization, on managing it with a customer focus, with customer being internal as well as external.

Consider the challenge of effecting process improvement, of creating change in the traditional organizational environment (culture). If we are fortunate, two or three departments may communicate well with each other. (Actually, it is the people within the departments who communicate and who cause or hinder progress.) Meaningful process improvement requires much broader involvement and participation. I am reminded of one of the first formal business process improvement accomplishments at Citizens Gas and Coke Utility (which we weren't ready to initiate until after more than five years of quality implementation effort). The process selected at first was thought to involve only a handful of departments. More complete analysis, however, revealed eight departments with 34 functional tasks actually involved in providing the service to the customer. We weren't trying to improve a process but were analyzing an entire subsystem, one having in the beginning three separate databases and a cycle time far beyond what we originally thought. The opportunity for reengineering is obvious, but it is extremely difficult to accomplish this in a nonquality environment because of the barriers within the traditional organization.

The new quality organization with a customer focus not only functions differently, and with greater potential, but its structure is different than the top-to-bottom organizational chart accommodates. Figure 2.2 illustrates how one might first attempt to show the quality organization using the most familiar technique. It fails, however, to convey the

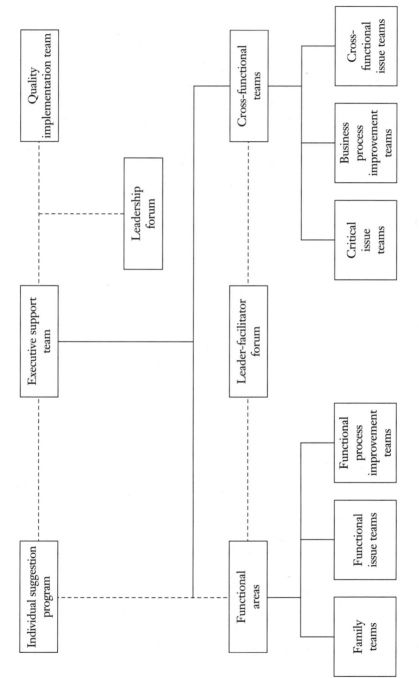

Figure 2.2. Management structure for a traditional quality environment.

nonvertical relationships of a quality environment and, in particular, the customer influence on everything.

Figure 2.3 more adequately depicts the makeup and activity of the customer-focused organization. Note that external or internal customer surrounds all else. Observe also that at the center of this universe is "executive support" which is what Part II will specifically discuss.

The broadest possible definition of customer and its potential goes beyond the organization as well. I have witnessed nearly amazing consequences when regulatory agencies, government, the public, and the community have been dealt with as customers. Not only does it provide opportunity for changing our relationships in some cases from adversarial to nonconfrontational, but often there is a much improved sense of purpose and direction. All of these not only benefit the organization, but considering these involvements with a customer focus enables all employees to relate and react with common purpose in their many varied contacts and activities.

Of course this does not mean that the customer focus is without conflict or frustration, because as already illustrated we individually and organizationally have many customers, far more than you might first think. In fact, when the executive management group at Citizens Gas and Coke Utility applied the methodology (the process) described in the next chapter, it identified 74 different customer groups it needed to serve. Obviously these groups couldn't be addressed all at once, so early in our journey we learned how to prioritize.

The pursuit of quality, of satisfying customer needs, doesn't make one's job easier—far from it. For me the past few years have been more challenging than all those preceding combined, but also far more rewarding and educational. Within this point is the fact that I've been privileged to be a part of an organizational transformation (one that is still occurring) where bottom-line results have been astounding in improved customer satisfaction, increased market share, safety, regulatory compliance, productivity, efficiency, and employee involvement in the pursuit of continual improvement. All of which is to say that although not easier, it has been and is worth it.

A true quality environment is driven by the customer focus. It provides our organizational direction as well as purpose. In it we can

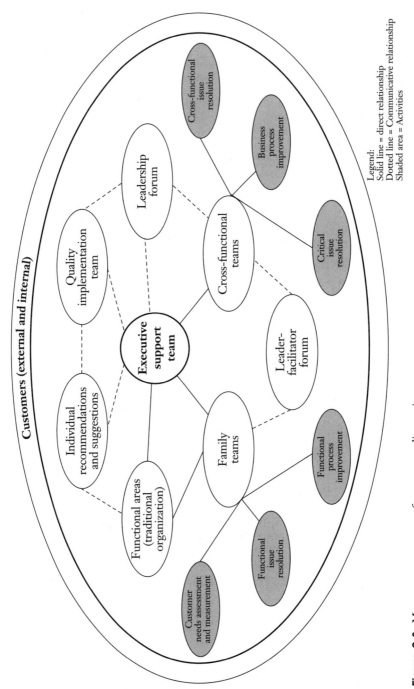

Figure 2.3. Management structure for a new quality environment.

identify the issues for which improvement strategies must be developed and the needs or expectations for which our delivery processes must be designed. It enables us to determine more correctly how the organization's resources should be applied. It provides the ability to establish measurements and performance indicators that are truly customer based and meaningful. It challenges conventional wisdom. It takes us away from old paradigms. It enables an organization to communicate and makes the strategic plan meaningful to all employees.

The pursuit of customer satisfaction doesn't mean the traditional organizational endeavors are not pursued or are subjugated. The customer focus provides the context in which and by which we do all we normally would do and more. It ensures that we improve the correct things, that we understand what is and isn't important. It is not another project or program, it is the foundation of all we do. It has its beginning but is never completed because the greater calling is not to meet customer needs and expectations, but to exceed them, thus ensuring success in the competitive marketplace. A quality environment is customer focused.

Note

1. B. Joseph White, "Accelerating Quality Improvement" (paper presented at the Total Quality Performance Conference, sponsored by the Conference Board), University of Michigan, January 21, 1988.

3 A Quality Environment Uses a Customer Satisfaction Methodology

A **process** *is required to ensure organization-wide consistency.*

A customer focus by itself is not enough to meet or exceed customer needs or expectations; that is, to implement quality. Management must provide the concepts, tools, and techniques necessary to accomplish this desired end. It is not a simple task. A quality organization has evolved to a level of understanding that recognizes it is a single total system comprised of several critical subsystems, each having many processes (for example, customer satisfaction, human resource utilization, issue resolution, policy development/deployment, planning, budgeting, and so on. In a traditional organization many of these would not be considered subsystems of a larger system each needing careful design, maintenance, and support, but they are and do. As the organization progresses in its quality pursuit, appreciation grows regarding the importance of understanding the interrelationships of its many activities.) Merely having a customer focus does not cause these to function in a manner beyond the traditional. It takes a process, an identifiable, understandable (organization-wide) methodology, framing various techniques to provide the structure for and direction of the quality pursuit.

This chapter is about a methodology, perhaps *the* methodology, that can make the difference between the few who succeed and the many more who fail in the quality journey. It begins with assessing customer requirements, then concentrates on the delivery mechanisms (the functional processes) necessary to provide them. The third phase measures the degree of satisfaction achieved, comparing this to what others similarly achieve for the purpose of identifying continual improvement opportunities. Figure 3.1 outlines this customer satisfaction process with its three phases.

A part of the second phase, delivery, is a six-step problem-solving or issue resolution process (Figure 3.2) that is used when the output (product, service, or activity) fails to meet the customer requirement. Note that in both its first two steps one is to consider customer aspects thereby maintaining the customer focus as the impact of the issue is identified and analyzed. This six-step graphic illustrates the potential for a major failing of traditional management as compared to those in a quality environment who possess the positive attribute of disciplined adherence to the six steps.

Traditional responses to issues and problems are targeted toward rapid decision making. The consequence of such an exercise may be to spend too little, if any, time in issue analysis and development of alternative solution strategies. The greatest failing in the old (though customary) tradition is the lack of customer impact consideration. This obviously leaves one vulnerable to applying tenets of old paradigms and to addressing and resolving issues from conventional wisdom or personal experience. The more senior one is in an organization, the more apt he or she is to approach needs or opportunities in this limited way.

Fundamental to what management in a quality environment has that is lacking in the traditional organization is the *discipline* necessary to maintain the customer focus, apply the three-phase customer satisfaction process, and, when needed, the six-step issue resolution technique. Organizations cannot afford to waste time and resources addressing issues of minimal customer priority or implementing wrong corrective strategies. Management in a quality environment is unrelenting in its ability to keep itself and the organization focused on the use of quality concepts, tools, and techniques. This fact in itself should provide ample

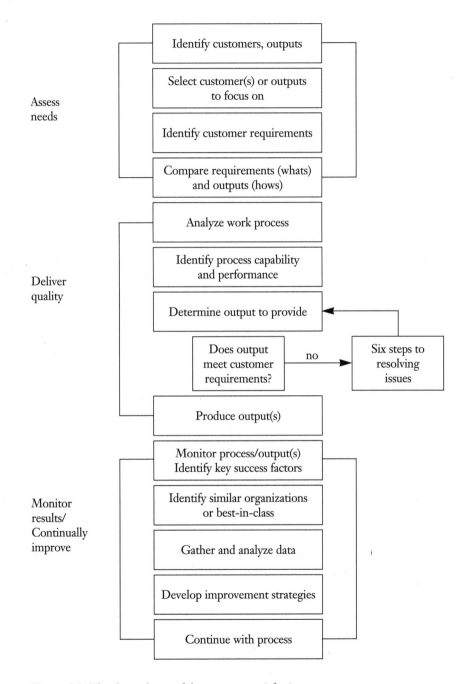

Figure 3.1. The three phases of the customer satisfaction process.

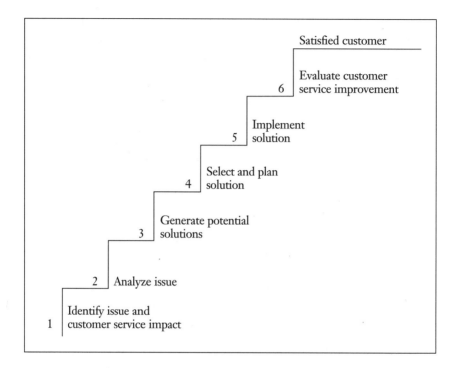

Figure 3.2. Six steps to resolving issues.

assurance that there remains much for management to do in a quality environment.

Many find greater comfort in the traditional way of managing because it is easier than being disciplined in maintaining the customer satisfaction focus and using its methodology. Implementing and maintaining a quality environment is not for the weak or faint of heart. Few organizations achieve their potential because too many people are too secure in their old ways and unwilling to commit and involve themselves. There are those, however, who are bold enough and wise enough to pursue and achieve, thereby gaining competitive advantage.

The challenges are great as well in ensuring use of the three-phase process, beginning with customer needs assessment. The importance of adhering to it cannot be overstated. Too many organizations fall short in their quality efforts because, though well intentioned, they fail to grasp the completeness or totality of the effort required. (I am being overly kind when I state "organizations fail" because the failure belongs to the management of the organization.) These failures are often the consequence of a process improvement focus without customer need assessment and consideration. This partial pursuit is seen by many in the organization as another management effort toward productivity improvement. In these cases not only does the positive rationale for improvement get lost, but the full improvement potential is not realized because the effort is restricted by departmental (functional) barriers and individual concerns regarding personal job security. When improvement efforts are based on better satisfying the customer, however, the barriers over time come down and serious consideration of improvement of the total system with all its functional components can begin. This happens as a result of those directly involved in performing the activities of the processes of the system seeing the improvement effort with a clearer, if not new, rationale. Companion to this must also be a new view by management of employees as customers too. (They are management's most important internal customer.) Consequently, addressing job security issues becomes a part of the process improvement activity.

Management must address other challenges as well if full improvement potential is to be realized. Concentration on process alone seems too often to be driven by a positive results mentality expected in too short a time frame, usually the traditional quarter-to-quarter yardstick. Frustration, impatience, and/or feelings of failure often accompany the too narrowly focused process improvement attempt, and the organization suffers rather than profits from the experience. Worse yet, the people directly involved with doing the process witness the shortcomings or ineptness of those directing the effort.

A similar fate awaits those who choose to focus their improvement effort on arbitrarily set targets (measurements) that are not customer derived. The truth is that too often we are measuring the wrong things, usually as a result of not having identified the customer requirements and their applicable measurements or from measuring elements of processes not appropriately linked to the customer.

The customer focus and the customer satisfaction process are intricately entwined and dependent on each other. They form the context for the improvement effort and provide the rationale and methodology for employee buy-in and involvement, thereby magnifying the results potential. They force the organization to think beyond departmental boundaries, to become cross-functional, to improve the entire system rather than only some parts of it. When this occurs, products and services can exceed customer expectation; value can be added without adding cost.

Although the importance of viewing employees as internal customers in process improvement was discussed in chapter 2, reemphasis of this point in the context of the customer satisfaction process is warranted. Just as when management applies the process to identify and address the needs and expectations of employees, so too can management use the process to improve individual outputs and departmentally contribute toward meeting the needs of the external customer. In a quality environment, management assures the focus stays on the customer and provides the methodology for continual improvement in meeting and exceeding customer needs.

The customer satisfaction process (methodology) is discussed in greater detail in the following pages, taken from my first book, *Implementing Quality With a Customer Focus*.

Develop Your Quality Process

The Customer Satisfaction Process

A quality mission statement and objectives alone are not enough to cause an organization to adopt a quality culture. A process must be developed that can be utilized to achieve the desires of the mission statement and targets of the objectives.

Discussion—perhaps even debate—must occur to determine what elements are necessary for the successful implementation of the quality process. Admittedly, there are different approaches as to what quality should be. Each organization must find its own comfort level regarding the elements and options that define how quality is to be achieved.

As I stated earlier, I believe customers and their needs should drive the process, and no matter where you are in the methodology, you must be able to relate to your customers. Work processes should have a customer basis; so, too, should our plan strategies. Problem solving should, in the first step of analysis, determine customer impact. Measurements should have an identifiable customer meaning as well. In all that we do, we should know who we're doing it for and what the need, real or perceived, is.

The customer satisfaction (that is, quality) process I advocate consists of three phases of activity (see Figure 3.1), assessment, delivery, and monitoring for continual improvement. For maximum success, the customer satisfaction process should be utilized by employees throughout the organization. Constant effort toward effective communication in support of the process is essential. Finally, a methodology must be present that permits disciplined resolution of problems, issues, and opportunities when they are encountered. These are the key elements of the customer satisfaction process, and they may be pursued by teams or by an individual.

Assessment

Needs assessment must not be done in the vacuum of conventional or personal wisdom. There is only one way to determine customer needs and that is to establish a communicative linkage and ask customers to identify their needs—real or perceived. As we assess needs, we need to identify our customers, and we need to list our outputs. In other words, "What do we do?" and "Who do we do it for?"

The list of customer and outputs will be long and confusing at the outset. Don't worry about where to begin, however. It really doesn't matter where you start. Logically, it makes sense to prioritize the list, identifying the three or four most important customers or outputs. It may be best, however, to select a relatively easy customer or output at first to develop a sense of how the process works. In any case, remember quality is a process with a beginning but no end. It has no time constraint because once started it is never completed. Our long lists, therefore, also will be worked on by those who follow in later years. We are only the beginning.

Having selected the customer or output, next determine the actual customer requirement. You can begin by establishing what you think the requirement is, but in every case you must *ask* the customer to identify or confirm the customer's actual need.

Finally, compare the requirements (the "what" you are to provide) with your outputs (the "how" you will provide). Now, analyze your findings, looking for needs with no outputs or outputs with no needs. Consider, too, whether there are measurements for the requirements which can be used later to determine how well you are performing and/or to establish a comparative basis for improvement strategies. Figure 3.3 shows the activities of the assessment phase and questions to ponder as you proceed through it.

Asking the customer what *really* is required also should provide data useful in prioritizing your outputs. Don't be surprised to find outputs not nearly as critical as assumed or specifications established upon misinterpreted needs. In some instances the output may be what the customer desires, but even here we need to proceed into the other phases of the process, studying the delivery mechanism and related measurements, always striving for ways to improve.

Delivery
Figure 3.4 describes the second phase of the process, which concentrates on delivery; that is, analyzing the work processes related to producing (providing) the output previously identified as required by the customer.

Study the various activities currently required to produce the output and consider their performance consistency and capability. It's important to contemplate this early in your pursuit whether you believe improvement opportunities exist or not.

Finally, determine the output your analysis indicates should be provided, comparing your recommendations to the identified customer requirement. There very well may be conflicts at this point because the output may not meet customer requirements, or the delivery capability may be restricted by procedures, standards, budgetary capabilities, or other obstacles. It is at this point we must force the consideration away from "why we can't" to "how we can." Discipline again must prevail, not only as a "can do" mind-set but in utilization of a systematic issue-resolution approach. We use the six-step methodology described in Figure 3.2 and strive to ensure we spend sufficient time in identifying

Customer Satisfaction Process Guide
—Assess Needs—

Activity	**Questions to consider**
Identify customers, outputs	Who are the customers?
	What do we provide?

List them all—there is no right or wrong answer!

Select customer(s) or output(s) to focus on	What criteria should be used?
	Who are the key customers?
	What are the key outputs?
	Do you have different types of customers?
	Have you discussed the results of this step with your team advisor?

If you are just starting, pick one—save the tough ones for later.

Identify customer requirements	Do you really know what the customer wants?
	Are there other needs that the customer has not stated?
	Have you negotiated the requirements with the customer?
	Have you reviewed current and past data?
	Do your customers all have the same needs?

Start with what you think is the customer's need, then ask the customer.

Compare requirements (whats) and outputs (hows)	Are there needs with no outputs?
	Are there outputs with no needs?
	Are there specifications or measures for the requirements?
	How does the customer feel you are doing?
	How does the customer rate you against the competition?
	How do you feel you are doing?

Organize the data and do some analysis.

Figure 3.3. First identify customer requirements.

Customer Satisfaction Process Guide
—Deliver Quality—

Activity	Questions to consider
Analyze work process	How do you produce the output?
	Can you diagram it?
Make sure you get into the details!	Are there other ways to do the job?
	Do others do it the same way?
	Do others do it differently?
	Can it be simplified?
	How do you know if you are doing a good job?
Identify process capability and performance	What is the process capable of providing?
	How consistent is the process?
You may need more data for this.	Can you always predict the results of the work?
Determine output to provide	Does the output meet customer requirements?
	If not, why not?
Test a few ideas—maybe first idea isn't best.	Have you discussed your results with your team advisor?
Product outputs	If there are changes needed, do you have a plan
Make changes	outlining how you will get them done (who, what, and when)?
Consider a pilot program or trial run.	Do you have everyone involved who needs to know about the changes?

Figure 3.4. Analyze data and implement the quality process to meet those requirements.

and analyzing the issue—or opportunity—and the customer-service impact (steps 1 and 2).

Too often the tendency is to begin by generating solutions or, worse yet, to select a solution without actually having done an analysis of the issue and its impact. Upper management may be more prone to this "hurried up" failure, convinced by their past experience—or current position—that they know what is best. When this happens we fail our organization in at least two ways: We haven't permitted proper analysis of the issue, and we haven't sought the ideas of others or listened to those offered. Obviously, such failure seriously affects the attitudes of those around us as well as limits the power of combining more than one idea with a thorough analysis of our options.

Monitoring

When output-and-requirement resolution is reached (and this may mean some degree of compromise may have been negotiated), the next step is to proceed with providing the output and begin the third part of the process: monitoring results and striving for continual improvement (see Figure 3.5). Since measurements are the vital elements utilized at this point, we must establish the key factors to reflect how successfully the delivery mechanism performs and how well we satisfy the customer's needs.

When measurement is driven by customer needs, tremendous opportunity for improvement may be found. Too often measurements have been established to provide well-intended productivity references but without regard to satisfactorily fulfilling the needs of our customers. For example, measuring the number of customer calls handled per hour by a customer service representative reveals nothing about whether the reason or issue was satisfactorily resolved. The more cost-effective measurement should recognize that more time spent in meeting the customer's needs in the beginning may mean less resolution time required by the organization overall. We must have this broader cross-functional appreciation for how our actions impact others, which is nothing more than seeing other individuals and departments as our internal customers.

Measuring against our own performance and striving to improve on it will provide a meaningful reward. I think even greater achievement

Customer Satisfaction Process Guide
—Monitor Results/Continually Improve—

Activity

Questions to consider

Monitor process/outputs
Identify key factors

How do you measure performance?
Where is improvement needed?
What does the team advisor think?
What should you monitor to guarantee that
    your product or service will continue to meet
    the needs of the customer?

> You need to gather enough data
> to give a clear picture.

Identify competitors or
best-in-class

Who is the best in marketing, finance, cost,
    quality, and delivery?

> First brainstorm possibilities,
> *then* narrow down.

Gather and analyze data

Can you improve the process or the output?
What have you learned from your competitors
    or others with similar processes?

> Get into more detail—
> reexamine cause-and-effect
> relationships.

Develop improvement strategy

What is your improvement target?
When and how do you plan to do it?
What help or resources will you need?
What are the action steps and timetable?
Are you continuing to monitor the process?

> Plan your work before working
> your plan!

Continue the process

What is the next priority?
Should you go into more detail on the
    same issue?
Should you pick other processes or outputs?

> What do you want to work on
> next?

Figure 3.5. Striving for continual improvement.

may be attained by studying those who provide similar outputs or do similar tasks. Often linkages can be formed where measurement data are exchanged, not for the sake of simply comparing numbers to numbers, but more importantly, to identify those who may be performing better than you. Once identified, the challenge is to determine *why* or *how* their delivery mechanism is different. From this analysis should come improvement strategies for becoming even better in meeting the needs of customers and doing so more effectively.

It's important to keep the organizational focus on the customer-satisfaction process and strive to make assessment, delivery of those needs, issue resolution, and measurement and continued improvement the routine way you go about your business rather than something extra or an afterthought. From the beginning, commit to be disciplined, almost unrelenting (in a quality sort of way) in use of the process.

4 In a Quality Environment There Is Commitment and Discipline

Quality doesn't just happen. Its implementation
requires ongoing dedication and support.
Achievement involves both the mind and the heart.

A customer focus and a methodology to support continual improvement of customer satisfaction are not enough in themselves to ensure a quality environment. Management must commit to the pursuit and be disciplined in adherence to its support of quality concepts and techniques. Successful implementation of quality involves the mind and the heart.

Bringing the entire inner self of the organization into the pursuit of a common goal is challenging to say the least. Perhaps dimensions of the soul seem too soft to practice or teach. Perhaps managerial philosophy appears at first glance to be a very personal, individual matter; it is and it isn't. For those who doubt or don't understand, take time to study the organizations that have succeeded in their quality quest. In each you will find visionary and inspirational leadership. You will find continuous commitment and disciplined pursuit of a quality environment.

This chapter is intended to emphasize emphatically the importance of commitment and discipline, and to illustrate their applicability to organizational success. What we in management must have is a better sense of very special individual attributes that we must try to learn, develop, and hone to enhance our ability to lead, manage, and support. A committed and disciplined organization begins with individual effort, and so too does it continue, sometimes through the sheer will power of those who understand the importance of achieving a quality environment.

I must emphasize the individual effort aspect. Regardless of the position held in management, we have inherited it from someone else, likely over many generations. Policies and practices are well established and long standing. Organizational processes and systems such as planning, budgeting, payroll, job evaluation, appraisals, compensation, and so on have been in place for many years. Standards and procedures are well defined and rigid. Authority levels are absolute. There is a hierarchy for power, control, and flow of information. The individual is part of an established, traditional organization. Implementing quality means all that is in place, all that has existed for years, is subject to change. It takes courage and fortitude to be in management in pursuit of a quality environment. It takes commitment and discipline, and these begin from within.

Change is never comfortable. It is disquieting and full of uncertainty. It is about newness, about uncharted waters. It is risky because certain initiatives or responses may not succeed or go as intended. There are obstacles that must be overcome. There are those who doubt and others who obstruct. Change is easiest it seems when it is forced by something external, when one must simply respond or react to it. Being a change agent, however, is quite different. It exposes one to question, to uncertainty, to new, untried ways. It makes one vulnerable. It requires us to sometimes say, "I don't know." To advocate change, to break from the past and from tradition, requires inner strength. It requires commitment and discipline.

Quality cannot be implemented single-handedly. It requires a team effort, beginning at the top, mobilizing all who are management and all who are the organization. This doesn't happen on command. The progress of understanding and acceptance of its responsibilities is slow, sometimes painfully so. In the early stages there will be but a handful leading, managing, and supporting, and prodding, pushing, and pulling the management group. This early effort will determine whether implementation will succeed, because it is management that will make or break the pursuit. Unless management itself can move from individuals competing for individual advancement and budgeted dollars to a collaborative team endeavor toward a common goal, a quality environment will not be achieved. Progress can be made even when but a few demonstrate by deed and example. The truly significant milestones occur, however, when the doubting or reluctant ones add their talents and determination to those of the original leaders.

Gentle persuasion is seldom enough to cause others to rethink and relearn. In the early days, we increased the ranks of advocates by first making quality a significant part of the management incentive plan, but even this still allowed some to merely go through the motions. Our people made us face what we were too slow in admitting; there are a handful who won't or can't get on board. The problem is that even though their numbers are few, they are of management, of those expected to lead. It is fairly easy to "talk the talk" rather than "walk the talk," and it's not uncommon for our employees to know first which we are doing. Commitment and discipline are required if this situation is to be handled in a manner supportive of the pursuit and consistent with the expectations of our employees, expectations based on the expressed intent by management to implement quality. When this issue is faced it impacts peer and subordinate, and the message of determination is absolute.

Commitment is so important it deserves further thought. What does this word mean? Webster's definition says it is "a pledge or promise to do something" and to commit is to "put to some purpose."[1] As I use it, the pledge, promise, and purpose is to constantly strive to meet and exceed customer expectations; that is, to establish and maintain the customer focus. As stated a moment ago this pledge, the commitment, begins first within oneself. Then, when verbalized, it is made to our employees and demonstrated in fact to our customers. As it is emphasized and reinforced it grows to an organization-wide attitude, a feeling that gives the organization its heart, soul, and spirit.

To consider commitment a managerial responsibility may seem unconventional to those who still hold to antiquated cold, calculating, unfeeling managerial approaches and practices. Yet those today who excel in quality management and have earned the right to be described as leaders have been able to establish a personal and organizational commitment to satisfying and exceeding customer needs.

Remember that customers are internal as well as external. We can improve most in satisfying external customers by meeting the needs of our internal customers, our employees. James Autry, president of the magazine group of the Meredith Corporation, publishers of the *Ladies Home Journal, Better Homes and Gardens,* and several other magazines, in his book *Love and Profit, The Art of Caring Leadership* provides managerial insights worth the attention of all who do or aspire to manage. In the book's introduction, he states, "Good management is largely a matter of love, or if you're uncomfortable with that word, call it caring, because proper management involves caring for people, not manipulating them."[2] He challenges us to

> approach management as a calling, a life engagement that, if done properly, combines technical and administrative skills with vision, compassion, honesty and trust to create an environment in which people can grow personally, can feel fulfilled, can contribute to a common good, and can share in the psychic, and financial rewards of a job well done.[3]

There it is, a mission statement for management, for paying attention to your internal customers to achieve the "common good" of satisfying and eventually exceeding external customer needs and expectations. This isn't "soft stuff" of which Autry writes and to which I refer; this is "gut stuff" and it can't be done without commitment, purpose, and discipline.

He goes on to say that

> Management, is in fact, a sacred trust in which the well-being of other people is put in your care during most of their working hours. It is a trust placed upon you first by those who put you in the job, but more important than that, it is a trust placed upon you after you get the job by those whom you are to manage.[4]

I have observed so many managers who in belief and practice always focus on the shareholder without understanding that without customers (the traditional kind) there won't be shareholders. So too without those customers there aren't employees. Around these simple truths we must recognize the system in which we work and with it the priorities and interdependencies. We must not ignore the needs of our employees because to do so lessens our ability to meet the needs and expectations of our customers and, consequently, the demands of the shareholder.

Responding to the needs of employees will, however, present management with many of the most challenging aspects of implementing quality. The truth is there will be times when it seems meeting external customer needs must be done at the expense of the internal customers. There will be conflicting demands. Improving processes to provide better products or services often will mean jobs are lost. A leaner organization also means a more limited career ladder. Fewer layers of managerial hierarchy means fewer promotional opportunities. Doing more with less has the potential for substantially increasing internal strife and individual stress. Implementing quality means change, and change is difficult for any of us to experience comfortably. It takes a special kind of management to lead, manage, and support the organization to a quality environment.

A quality environment is about commitment to establishing and maintaining a customer focus; viewing employees and functional departments as customers; a step-by-step methodology for pursuing, meeting, and exceeding customer needs and for resolving issues; and caring about your employees yet never losing the external customer focus. These require great organizational and great individual strength. It is important to recognize and remember that it is an environment created not by accident but by deed. Focus, methodology, commitment, and caring even when combined still will not ensure a quality environment. Another essential ingredient is discipline, another responsibility of management to establish and maintain.

Webster's definition of discipline is "self-control, enforcing obedience, a system of rules."[5] When applied to the organizational setting, discipline means requiring management to show the way and to stay on course. Perhaps one of the comforts in traditional managerial approaches is that they are of such short duration that they don't require discipline or endurance or the open scrutiny by one's employees. In a quality environment management must expect to be tested often. Its culture requires total commitment and a strict adherence to its rules and its system. It requires a discipline, for which management is responsible.

Quality cannot be implemented without commitment and discipline. Eight years into implementing quality, I still found some of the most difficult challenges. These can simply be described as changing old ways to new, both individually and organizationally. Change is never easy. It is never without risk, uncertainty, and challenge. Positive change can only be effected if there is a special spirit in the way it is approached. Such spirit comes from commitment to the principles of quality and disciplined adherence to their pursuit.

Notes

1. *Webster's New World Dictionary of the American Language, Second College Edition*, ed. David B. Guralnik (New York: The World Publishing Company, 1972), 286.

2. James A. Autry, *Love and Profit, The Art of Caring Leadership* (New York: William Morrow and Company, 1991), 13.

3. Ibid., 14.

4. Ibid., 15.

5. *Webster's New World Dictionary of the American Language*, 401.

5 In a Quality Environment There Is Teamwork

There is, I think, great misunderstanding about
people working together to improve their outputs.

Management has not studied enough the topic of teams and teamwork, and, consequently, there is considerable misunderstanding and confusion around the topic. In these next pages I will discuss what we have experienced at Citizens Gas and Coke Utility regarding teamwork and its importance to effecting a quality environment. In particular I hope to emphasize further that it is the organizational environment, the culture, the climate, for which management is most responsible. Teamwork must be seen as a strategic milestone in the evolution toward a quality environment. We must also recognize that the traditional organization and the way it operates (that is, the way it is managed) hinders, if not obstructs, achievement of the desired total quality state.

It is the desired state of the organization that we should first understand, then we can establish the action plan. The organization must state in its quality mission statement its intent and how this will be achieved. The organization's goals should be reviewed over and over again as the journey continues. Citizens Gas and Coke Utility's mission statement, written seven years ago, remains as originally stated (Figure 5.1) and has

Mission Statement: The quality mission of Citizens Gas and Coke Utility is to satisfy the needs of our customers, both internal as well as external. Together we will create and maintain an environment where all are motivated toward the satisfaction of customer needs, each contributing his or her own unique talents and abilities to the process. Through mutual respect, personal pride, and teamwork, we will strive for excellence—continually improving our services, processes, and products. We will work to be the best at what we do, in every phase of our business at every level.

Figure 5.1. Citizens Gas and Coke Utility quality process.

helped guide and remind us of what we pursue. In it, we first state our purpose ("to satisfy the needs of our customers, both internal as well as external") then *how* it will be achieved. Note that the first aspect addressed is creation of the appropriate environment. Now observe the most critically important dimension of the entire statement, the fact that achieving the mission is predicated on doing it together. There is no delineation of responsibilities; throughout, the pursuit actions are stated in the plural, recognizing they will only be achieved if "we" do them. There is, however, no mention of teams, only teamwork.

Teamwork, like customer satisfaction, is something the organization must strive to achieve. It also doesn't happen by command or within a short time. It takes place toward the end of the journey, and it requires an action plan specifically directed toward its accomplishment. Management must consider what is necessary for teamwork to be achieved. Part of this consideration is the recognition of those things that limit, hinder, and obstruct its realization. Throughout this book references are made to these organizational limitations, but they can be summarized as being of the traditional structure, styles, and practices that must be changed if a quality environment is to be achieved. They are about the organization in which departments compete against departments, individuals against individuals. They are about management systems and processes that require and encourage competition rather than collaboration, that reflect how the game is to be played to win and get ahead. If you doubt or question this, think about how the traditional organization plans, budgets, communicates, empowers, delegates, develops its human resource, and compensates.

There is much management must change to make teamwork a fact. Using teams to identify customer needs and the processes necessary to meet and exceed them provides a way to start the functional units of the organization toward greater collaboration, both employee to employee and department to department. Likewise, cross-functional teams (made up of individuals from various functions or departments) can be used to address organizational issues and improvement opportunities. It is important to recognize that teams are not an end in themselves; they are a *vehicle* to take us toward the goal of teamwork.

There is much management must do to lead, manage, and support team activity appropriately. These needs will be discussed in Part II. Here I will describe further the evolutionary nature of teamwork as we have experienced it at Citizens Gas and Coke Utility. Our experiences are consistent with the findings published in 1992 by the American Quality Foundation and Ernst & Young in *The International Quality Study Best Practices Report, An Analysis of Management Practices that Impact Performance.* In the report 945 management practices of over 580 organizations in four industries on three continents are analyzed. The practices are studied in terms of relative performance associated with profitability, productivity, and quality, and from these higher-, medium-, and lower-performance categories are determined. The report is full of useful information, but there may be a tendency for the hurried reader not to grasp that performance itself evolves over time as do the practices from the lower category to the higher. The findings reflect that the higher-performing organization's use of teams to help performance is not as important as it is to the lower-performing organizations. I believe that is because the higher-performing organization has reached the point where teamwork has become an ethic practiced routinely.[1]

Webster's defines teamwork as "joint action by a group of people in which individual interests are subordinated to group unity and efficiency."[2] As I read this definition I was reminded of the comments of a member of one of our early teams when asked to describe some of the difficulties the team had experienced. "At first," he stated, "it seemed we weren't getting anywhere, that all we were doing was arguing about what each of us thought was the best idea. Then we realized that it wasn't what 'I wanted' that was important, but what was best, in general, for the group, the organization. Then we began to make progress!" Teams provide a forum where such realization can occur, but much more than permission to exist must be present. There must be a focus easily understood as to why the team exists and a methodology as to how it should proceed.

There are many ingredients for the quality environment recipe, and they must be carefully measured and mixed. There must be consistency and organization-wide commonality. The customer focus, customer satisfaction process, commitment, discipline, and teamwork provide part of what is necessary, but they only occur if management understands and fulfills its role, if we know how to lead, manage, and support. We must change our attitudes and actions if the people and the organization are to change theirs.

Quality doesn't happen overnight. It evolves over a long period of time. It is achieved in a step-by-step fashion. Sometimes the progress is forward and visible, other times it seems we're not progressing at all or have gone backwards. It takes great patience to achieve the quality environment. Look again at the quality mission statement in Figure 5.1: "Through mutual respect, personal pride, and teamwork, we will strive for excellence—continually improving our services, processes, and products." Bringing the organization from the traditional belief that each of us need only to fulfill our own specific job to one striving to continually improve on the way we do the job is a tremendous undertaking and it can only be attained by individuals engaging in the effort together. I'm reminded of the words of one of our employees who stated the beautifully simplistic truth, "Working together really does work!"

Several times I have referred to the evolutionary nature of the quality journey. It is shown clearly in the organization's movement from teams to teamwork. The aspect of evolution is in itself critically important to understand and accept. The next chapter is devoted solely to this subject and how in our quality implementation the pace of the effort and our expectation must be slow and methodical. Organizational growth to a mature state of people working together, to an environment of teamwork, takes time. As stated in the beginning of this chapter, it also takes a well-developed and applied action plan to make it happen.

I have seen teams succeed and fail, progress nicely and flounder. I have gone through the trials of misunderstanding and misdirecting team activity, of well-intended but not well-orchestrated teamwork pursuit. Most often the difficulty was due either to taking management almost totally out of the equation or to lack of managerial expertise in support of teamwork. I believe teams are the way you bring the organization to a state of teamwork, but to achieve this desired end, management must be directly involved and must know what to do and how to do it. The common direction for such effort is found in the customer focus, and the customer satisfaction methodology provides the process. These alone, however, will not ensure success. Teams (and eventually teamwork) require the previously mentioned, extremely important ingredient of managerial support.

The subtitle of this book acknowledges support as an equal ingredient of management in a quality environment. Nowhere is its importance more clearly demonstrated than in using teams to achieve teamwork. Support is not visible. Its definition reflects its special nature "to bear the weight of; to give courage, faith, or confidence to; to help or comfort; to give approval to or be in favor of; to maintain and provide for."[3] I especially like the following parts of the definition: "to bear; endure; submit to; tolerate." They describe attitudes and conditions of our managerial psyche usually thought not to be required of us.

Teamwork occurs only with the careful nurturing of management. It requires us to change many of our ways, which will be illustrated in subsequent pages. For now, let it suffice to say that teamwork can only be achieved when management holds it ever so gently. Just as Figure 5.2 illustrates, it takes direction, guidance, support, encouragement, patience, and responsiveness from management. It is a condition that only we can create, or, if we have been fortunate enough to have inherited it, only we can maintain. Like all else in the quality environment, it is achieved one step at a time and its rewards for the organization are well worth the effort required.

Figure 5.2. Teamwork is not hands-off but hands-on—ever so gently.

Notes

1. American Quality Foundation and Ernst & Young, *The International Quality Study Best Practices Report, An Analysis of Management Practices That Impact Performance* (Cleveland, Ohio: Ernst & Young and New York: American Quality Foundation, 1992).

2. *Webster's New World Dictionary of the American Language, Second College Edition,* ed. David B. Guralnik (New York: The World Publishing Company, 1972), 1459.

3. Ibid., 1431.

6 The Quality Environment Evolves Over Time

*Quality itself is a process, having a beginning
but no ending. It should not be thought of
as a program or project to be completed within
a fixed time frame.*

Several times in the preceding chapters I have made reference to different facets of quality evolving over time. Indeed, implementing quality is an evolutionary process. This point is so important it deserves a chapter of its own to ensure that the reader doesn't assume otherwise, a totally natural risk given our penchant for immediacy.

Evolution applies to every aspect of quality implementation. It is attained by a step-by-step progression, one of walking before running, of modest success before major success. This requires a special understanding by management. It requires great patience and a mind-set very different than our typical by-the-end-of-next-quarter-or-fiscal-year mentality. Implementing quality is not a separate activity; it is not something done in addition to other organizational tasks. It is about everything the organization does, all that it is about, and the way everything is done. As I look back over what we've done at Citizens Gas and Coke Utility over the past seven years and ahead to what we must still accomplish, it is accurate to say we will have addressed all that we are about. Yet we didn't set out to do change for change's sake.

All that has occurred and will occur in future years has been a natural progression toward satisfying and exceeding customer needs and expectations, of continually improving our organizational processes toward this end, and of making all organizational parts function as one. The International Quality Study previously referenced points to our inability to grasp the progressive, evolutionary nature of moving from low to mid to high organizational performance levels. It challenges the "proponents of quality improvement [who] advocate a general quality model thought to be universally beneficial."[1] It then continues,

> Included are such practices as:
>
> - Focusing on teams as the basic structure of work.
> - Empowering everyone in the workforce.
> - Making heavy use of the standard "quality tools."
> - Benchmarking against the "best of the best."
> - Letting the "voice of the customer direct the development of new products and services."
> - Designing quality into your products and services rather than trying to "inspect it in."[2]

The study is correct in causing us to understand that practices and their impacts vary from performance level to performance level, but my experience causes me to believe that the variance is a natural outcome of the organization evolving from its original state to its new, from the traditional, functional, hierarchial entity to the singularly orchestrated total system. A snapshot taken at any point in time will not depict what you will be doing later in the quality journey.

In each of the previous chapters the topic described changes in its state and occurrence as implementation progresses, as the activity matures. The customer satisfaction focus evolves from concept to deed and routine practice. The satisfaction process or methodology, though in basic form remaining, becomes less identifiable as the organization moves from simple sequential application to flexible utilization beginning at any point in its three phases or six steps, yet considering all others. Commitment and discipline go through distinctly observable changes as they are by necessity at first almost forced on management consciousness to the time they exist naturally and comfortably within those who manage. Finally, teamwork does not spring forth from any model. It evolves, beginning with teams, but only if many other evolutionary changes occur too.

In many ways explaining "Why?" is the beginning of the quality pursuit. It appears first as we try to convey what quality is about and why it is important. Although one might think this conveyance is an organizational challenge, it deals almost exclusively with management, particularly those managers at the top of the organization. Unless the organization is in dire straits, many in executive positions are the least likely to embrace the need to change. Executives are comfortable with where they are and how they got there. It is for this reason that so few organizations pursue quality and even fewer are successful.

The "Why?" factor isn't found only as it relates to management, however. It applies to every task done in the organization. In the traditional organization little time is spent with why a task is to be done. Instead, training is based on what to do. Some may even respond, as I once did, if asked "Why?" with "Because I told you so!" Without a proper response to "Why?" or without including an explanation of why the task is important how can one possibly learn all there is to know? In particular, how can one possibly improve on the tasks and do the job better? If we are going to satisfy and eventually exceed customer needs, outdistance the competition, respond effectively to or anticipate change, we must be sure the organization properly responds to the "Why?" factor. This is the only way every task and every process can be continually improved.

Responding to "Why?" is an individual matter. Consequently, it takes time to effect. This is the reason it so often isn't done, but it is also why successful quality implementation is evolutionary. It cannot, however, be left to chance; it must be taught, over and over again. Humans learn through repetition. We need to remember this as we study and try to learn, and as we teach or have our organization teach.

There needs to be a structure provided to cause the natural consideration of why things are done. Figure 6.1 shows again the customer satisfaction methodology described in chapter 3. What it contains is the structure to ensure that "Why?" is addressed. When we look at our processes, that is, the second, deliver, phase, we must ensure that there is a customer requirement and we know what it is. In essence, we are asking, "Why are we doing what we're doing?" Figure 6.2 repeats the six-step problem-solving methodology also from chapter 3. Steps one through three in it cause us to answer "Why?" a particular strategy should be implemented. In a later chapter I'll describe how we changed our individual appraisal system to one based on personal performance planning. It provides the structure for the manager to respond to "Why?" for each nonbargaining employee. All of these help bring the organization to a total quality environment or condition or state, but concept and technique must be learned before they can be effectively practiced. Here again the evolutionary nature of quality implementation is present.

Before starting our quality effort nearly all learning in our company was task based. People were trained to perform specific tasks. Generally, we taught how something was to be done with little attention to why the tasks were important and their relationship to larger processes. Quality has changed much of the way we teach. It has brought a sense of curriculum to what must be known about the organization and, with it, education in how we learn. Here too, the evolving nature of our progression is demonstrated. We no longer believe a one-time exposure teaches as now we train and educate. We also understand that there are certain subjects that are universal in their importance to the organization. All of us are expected to always be learning, to always try to improve ourselves so to improve the organization, which too is always evolving.

The quality curriculum evolves over time as new needs are identified and responses to them developed. In our case we began with only two courses. Quality Education 1 (QE 1) was basic education in quality concepts and techniques taught to the entire organization. Companion to it was training for team leaders and facilitators (QE 2). Today, we have QE 3, a refresher in concepts and techniques but elevated to organizational

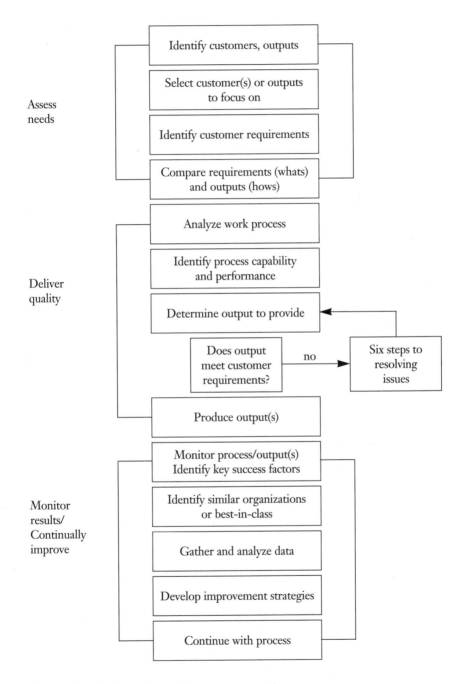

Figure 6.1. The three phases of the customer satisfaction process.

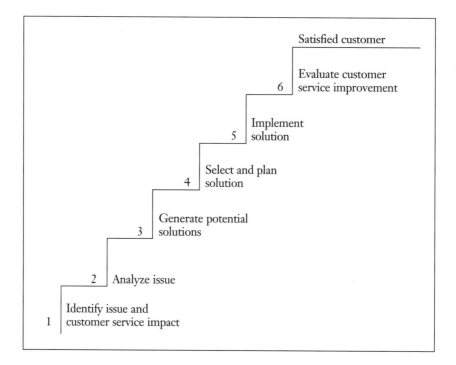

Figure 6.2. Six steps to resolving issues.

and individual pursuit of continual improvement; QE 4, training in measurement techniques; QE 5, education about organization values and their application in attaining the mission, vision, and goals of the organization; and several learning modules about leadership. There will be more added to this list because, in the quality environment, one is always learning.

Pacing the development of the organization, responding to the "Why?" factor, providing the necessary structure, encouraging the development of an ever-maturing education, and training curriculum all require a special kind of management. These require understanding, skill, and patience. They evolve over time, but perhaps we can expedite the evolution now that you better understand what a quality environment is, by sharing thoughts about management in a quality environment.

Notes

1. American Quality Foundation and Ernst & Young, *The International Quality Study Best Practices Report, An Analysis of Management Practices That Impact Performance* (Cleveland, Ohio: Ernst & Young and New York: American Quality Foundation, 1992).

2. Ibid., 6.

7 The Quality Environment Requires a New Type of Management

*In a quality environment traditional management
approaches and structure change to complement
cross-functional as well as functional activities,
team as well as individual pursuits.*

The previous chapters have described key elements of a quality environment, but they only occur through management action—through leadership, management, and support. Understanding what quality is and isn't, establishing a customer focus, using a customer satisfaction methodology, being committed and disciplined, pursuing teamwork, and pacing the pursuit so that it evolves are all dependent on management knowing not only what must be done but how to make it happen. Fundamental to this occurring is the requirement for management to change individually and collectively.

It has only been a few years, since the beginning of our quality journey, that I have begun to be a student of management theory and practice, but even then only as they apply to the actual needs of our organization. This writing shares what I've learned and is in many ways a chronicle of my personal managerial transformation so far. This is important to understand because what I've already shared and what

55

follows isn't theoretical; it is what has actually occurred. We have already experienced a tremendous change in the way we manage the company, and in personal managerial style and attitude. We have seen and are seeing organizational and operational processes and systems change; yet this is not what we set out to do. Our intent was and is to satisfy the needs of our customers, both external and internal. This is the catalyst for organizational change and for managerial transformation.

The customer focus expands the view of management; it takes us beyond simple task performance and functional competency; it takes us to cross-functional organizational considerations; it causes us to better deal with today's issues and prepare for those of tomorrow; it takes us to the future. As already explained, companion to the customer focus is the customer satisfaction methodology, the process for effecting the change. We began at the top of the organization, forming a team with the CEO as team leader and his direct reports as team members. We identified our outputs (see chapter 6) and then the customer involved. The real beginning occurred, however, when, for the first time, we began considering the outputs in the context of customer needs as described by the customer and not by us.

In those first steps we listed more than 100 different outputs of the team. These were grouped under the categories of culture, internal communication, external communication, human resources, policy, leadership, control, and planning. It is worth noting that the single largest category was by far that of control, which today is dramatically changed. The other categories have also had their related outputs substantially altered as customer need has been realized and processes redesigned to meet the need. To illustrate, I'll describe changes that have occurred in communications, human resources, and planning. Changes in all categories will be obvious in later chapters as the entire managerial job description is defined.

One of the first cross-functional teams (a team comprised of employees from various functional departments) we chartered was one to recommend communicative needs necessary to support quality implementation. Its findings and recommendations were all based around the fact that information was not shared other than on a need-to-know basis. Its efforts were focused on practices of management to employees, departments to departments, and employees to employees. Today I realize the guarding of information was most commonly found in yet another group as well, and that was management to management.

These findings shouldn't be surprising since, in the traditional organization, information is power, and the more you know the more the organization depends on you. A new paradigm of open communication and freely flowing information, however, is required in a quality environment. As this evolves, the organization becomes less competitive and more collaborative. It takes the organization from a functional mode to a cross-functional teamwork type. It becomes the foundation on which business process improvement can and does occur.

Before management can cause this transformation elsewhere in the organization, it must first get its own act together. There was a time when the strategic plan at Citizens Gas and Coke Utility was developed by and known by only five top-level managers. Today we share it with all employees. Not very long ago executive staff would meet weekly for an around-the-table updating of what was transpiring in one's area of responsibility. It was not uncommon for these sharings to be guarded conveyances of the good-news-only variety. After all, negative happenings in "my" area were mine to worry about and handle; they were not to be shared openly and possibly reflect badly on my managerial competency. When our internal customers, our employees, told us one of their greatest needs was for us to improve our leadership style, we learned (eventually) that central to our improvement were issues of trust and openness. These improvement opportunities began in our own relationships with each other and our direct reports, and then rippled throughout the organization. The improvement was about what and how we communicated.

Changes in attitudes and practices about human resource utilization also give testimony to management's development in a quality environment. When we began, human resource matters were what the personnel department handled. Today most of what I do is directly or indirectly related to caring for the human resource. The changes we have witnessed have resulted from using the customer satisfaction process, the three-phase methodology, to identity the needs of our employees (internal customers), the delivery mechanisms (processes) for meeting the needs, and the measurements that indicate how well needs are being met and most importantly where improvement opportunities are. The improvements we have experienced and are experiencing have resulted from the efforts of the now titled human resources department, working in concert with management and led by the executive support team (our CEO and his direct reports). Perhaps the greatest improvements, however, have resulted from individuals in management (like me) who now think of their direct reports as customers rather than subordinates.

The improvement needs (opportunities) of the organization's human resource, our employees, will rather consistently be found to be regarding antiquated delivery systems (processes) and equally antiquated managerial styles and behaviors. In all instances, these are controlled or influenced by management, not the employee. They form the environment in which work is done. Figure 7.1 lists the topical areas of employee needs that frame most of what this book is about. In my early quality development I don't believe I realized the inner relationships of the topics with each other; today I see them as related processes making up a single human resource delivery system. It is also imperative to realize that these needs are not topics to which other functions, departments, or individuals must respond. They require one's personal involvement.

More trust
More empowerment
Decision making too high
Inadequate individual appraisals
Poor communications
Limited personal growth opportunities
No career counseling
Management systems inconsistent with quality

Figure 7.1. Employee needs/human resource issues.

Quality has had no greater impact on me than in its requirement for changing my personal managerial styles, habits, and attitudes. Before quality, I used the human resource to perform tasks, and to get the job done. Today beyond task fulfillment is the challenge of improving the way tasks are fulfilled, and this requires providing improvement opportunities for my direct reports. I strive not to be the boss, but coach and teacher; to take the time to explain why the tasks are to be done, to share information, and, very importantly, to facilitate the development of the individual. Chapter 17 is devoted entirely to the tool we use for individual development. It describes the personal planning and review process (PPR) that materialized from redesigning our old-world appraisal process in response to the needs of our employees. Figure 7.2 illustrates other leadership, management, and support human resource related pursuits for which I'm responsible as I work toward creating and maintaining a quality environment.

To this point I've illustrated changes in the outputs of communications and human resources experienced as we have evolved toward a quality environment by responding to customer needs. You will observe transformation elements of each of these throughout the book because they are essential in all management does. To this I'll add another process, planning, that has been redesigned as the result of the natural progress of our efforts. Chapter 3 described in detail what is now known as the planning and resource allocation process, but a general overview

Focuses on the customer	Understands and shares mission, vision, and values
Develops direct reports	Walks the talk
Coaches/teaches	Practices open communication
Leads by example	Stresses honesty
Has integrity	Is self-disciplined
Appreciates human values	Tries new ideas
Is flexible	Delegates
Is team-oriented	Trusts

Figure 7.2. Leadership, management, and support attributes.

of this changed managerial output further illustrates how management can improve by responding to customer needs.

Before quality, planning and budgeting were very separate processes; today they are one. Before, involvement in them was on a selective and/or functional (departmental) basis; today, all levels of management are involved and the activity is both functional and cross-functional, involving employees from traditional departments as well as teams. Before, related information was provided on a need-to-know basis; today, it is universally shared. Today we understand the specifics of the planning and resource allocation process provide the answers to the Why? question and the foundation on which organization-wide improvement effort must be based. Today we strive to have all employees aware of the plan and its contents. The changes witnessed have been dramatic, yet they have occurred a step at a time. They have occurred by ensuring that one's outputs are consistent with customer needs. They have occurred by continually trying to improve.

The management responsibilities in a quality environment are much broader than those in a traditional organization because both external and internal customer needs must be addressed. The structural depiction used in chapter 2 is again provided here (Figure 7.3) with only its heading changed. Chapter 19 describes in detail the managerial components of the quality environment, but for here note that functional area (traditional organization) responsibility is only a part of a bigger system. In it management's activities change as does the structure of the organization. This brings us to the subject intended: management in a quality environment.

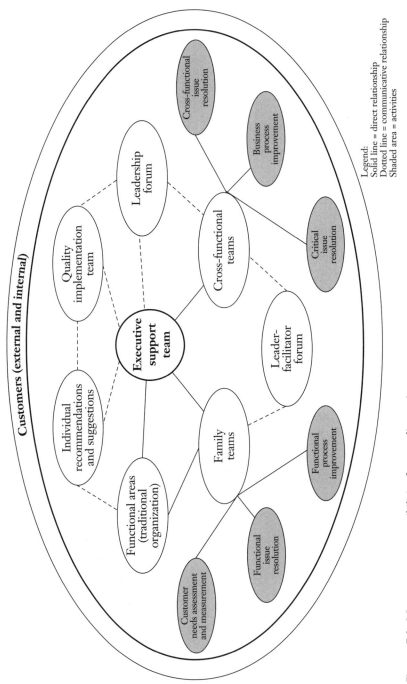

Figure 7.3. Management responsibilities for a quality environment.

Part II:
Management
(in a Quality Environment)

8 Seeing Management as a System

*We need a better understanding of what
it is we are to do as management. We need to
rethink our job description.*

Until becoming part of the quality implementation effort in our company, I had a narrow concept of management, probably best described as how to get others to accomplish what I wanted done. Today my understanding has been considerably broadened through the experience of quality, of striving to improve on meeting customer needs. Previously, I had little appreciation for my responsibilities beyond the specific functions for which I was responsible. My job description, as were all others, described my duties function by function, task by task. It emphasized authority and control. It essentially defined "my" territory. Today I recognize that what I am to do must be in concert with a total management system.

To better comprehend the implications of the just stated fact consider the following definitions. First from *Webster's New World Dictionary:* "system: a set of things so related as to form a unity or organic whole."[1] To this, add, from the *Encyclopedia of Professional Management:* "the most comprehensive definition (of management) views management as an integrating process by which authorized individuals create, maintain, and operate an organization in the selection and accomplishment of its aims."[2] Later, it lists five basic concepts of management and selects the following as the most fundamental:

> Management is the performance of the critical functions essential to the success of an organization. Management can usefully be viewed as a network of interrelated functional responsibilities. They are not a sequence of activities but rather a set of interacting activities that constitute a whole. It should be recognized that activity in one function has impact on one or more of the other functions.

Management must therefore be seen, I believe, as a system.

Traditional managerial practices based on function-by-function concepts limit our appreciation of the interrelationships. Too often they cause competition rather than collaboration. To illustrate, think about how we have traditionally performed the budgeting process, causing departmental competition for the limited dollar resource. Think also about information sharing or, more correctly stated, lack of sharing in the traditional organization where information is given on a need-to-know basis. We too did these things before quality, but we have gradually evolved toward an organization appreciating the interrelationships of our various functions and toward understanding the total system.

It was the concept of the internal customer that has caused our evolution and the changes in our management system. Although previously stated, it is worth further emphasis to fully appreciate how dramatically practices, techniques, and styles change when individual and departmental outputs are thought of in terms of satisfying the customers' needs. This instantly took us beyond our functional boundaries, began our examination of delivery processes (often including members of other departments), and initiated the breakdown of functional barriers.

All of this began first at the executive level, where, by necessity, such change must begin. As I describe management in a quality environment, my emphasis will be primarily on the top of the organization—the executive—because it is here that the organization's environment, its culture, is determined. It is here that leadership, management, and support begin.

Figure 8.1 presents the activity description for Citizens Gas and Coke Utility's executive support team (our CEO and his direct reports). It can be thought of as our job description, but recognize that the job requirements are collective rather than singular. They are for the team in support of the organization. The activities identified should be

A. Create and maintain a quality environment (culture)
- Mission
- Vision
- Values
- Quality focus
- Quality methodology/techniques
- Communication
- Priorities/expectations
- Performance indicators/results
- Recognition
- Education/training

B. Manage and support quality process
- Cross-functional team support
- Assign advisors
- Review/approve charters
- Provide tools/techniques
- Analyze status reports
- Recommendations follow-up/implementation

C. Coordinate/facilitate planning—resource allocation process
- Goals/objectives
- Priorities
- Budget ($) parameters
- Communication to employees
- Departmental/individual linkages

D. Develop and implement policy
- Human resources
- Improving customer satisfaction
- Organization structure
- Organization's strategic issues
- Leadership improvement

E. Coordinate/facilitate customer satisfaction pursuit
- Priority external customers (traditional)
- Priority external customers (nontraditional)
- Internal customers

F. Teach/coach/mentor/develop
- Functional area(s)
- Tasks
- Quality concepts/technology
- Walk the talk
- Direct reports
- Information
- Rationale (why things happen)

Figure 8.1. Executive support team activity description.

thought of in the context of the quality organization and responsibility chart shown in the previous chapter (Figure 7.3). In it note again that executive support is at the center of the universe, at the heart of the organization. (For purposes of our discussion here, the activities identified are all internally focused and do not include those externally related, that is, community, government, and so on.)

Analysis of the two graphics should indicate that there is much more to management in a quality environment than the traditional functional responsibilities, although those exist as well. They frame what must be done and a structure for doing it. The executive support team activities describe what management should be about and are the substance of this book. The succeeding chapters will examine each in more detail, but first a few more thoughts about management as a system.

There are many management processes that make up the management system. Referring to Webster's again, a process is "a particular method of doing something, generally involving a number of steps or operations."[3] I believe this continuation of the definition is appropriate: "a continuing development involving many changes." Management must be dynamic and alert to changing needs and conditions. A process cannot be performed as though the future will be the same as today. Management must recognize that the way something was done yesterday may not respond to today's needs. Yet organizations still rely on standards, procedures, and policies as though written in stone. The concept of continual improvement of management processes and, consequently, the management system, is vital to the success and perhaps the survival of the organization.

Again and again the customer focus and the customer satisfaction methodology provide the catalytic agents for dynamic management. They provide the process to improve the process. They also provide the structure to what otherwise might be or appear to be unstructured. They provide consistency where management might otherwise be inconsistent. In the past, I've witnessed and led well-intended efforts that I expect the employees viewed more in a program-of-the-month manner than as steps toward a single destination. These, at best, were hit-or-miss endeavors and clearly lacked a common foundation. As one might expect, their appeal and acceptance were limited. All of this began to change with our pursuit of a total quality environment. We have learned that every function of the organization fits within the customer satisfaction focus and its methodology, that every activity can utilize quality techniques, and that every employee can be part of the effort. There are still programs and new strategies that evolve in response to ever-changing customer needs, but quality now provides a common linkage to what otherwise might be disjointed. Managers must understand that it is our responsibility to ensure there is commonality in what is done, to provide consistency, to provide structure, and to provide a total system in which many processes interrelate.

As we move through the next chapters it is important to grasp their interrelationships and to see them as parts of a total system. They are the to-do list for management in a quality environment. Though their actions begin at the top of the organization, their resultant outputs ripple to its boundaries and frame all that it is and will be. It is appropriate to list them one time as a single sentence so to see them together rather than separately. Management in a quality environment must create and maintain a quality environment (culture), manage and support the quality process, coordinate and facilitate the planning/resource allocation process, develop and implement policy, coordinate and facilitate priority customer satisfaction pursuits, and teach/coach/mentor and communicate with the traditional functional areas of the organization.

Notes

1. *Webster's New World Dictionary of the American Language, Second College Edition*, ed. David B. Guralnik (New York: The World Publishing Company, 1972), 1445.

2. *Encyclopedia of Professional Management* (New York: McGraw-Hill, 1978), 640.

3. *Webster's New World Dictionary*, 1133.

9 Create and Maintain a Quality Environment (Culture)

*The most important aspect of management
is the environment or culture we create and, once
created, maintain. It determines how the workforce
will view what it does, why it does it, and how
tasks should be done.*

When we began implementing quality we had no real understanding of what we had started. We didn't fully appreciate that we would over time dramatically change the environment in which we all work—and with it the organization's culture. What I share has evolved, not in response to the admonishment to create and maintain a quality environment, but rather in response to meeting the needs of our internal customers: our employees.

Figure 9.1 identifies the components of the environment, the activities and processes that management must, and will, address. The first four, mission, vision, values, and quality focus, provide the purpose, direction, principles, and clarity for all the organization is about and does. Figure 9.2 repeats the single system illustration from chapter 2, this time to depict how these elements help form the structure for the organization. The quality focus is the target of satisfying and exceeding,

• Mission	• Communication
• Vision	• Priorities/expectations
• Values	• Performance indicators/results
• Quality focus	• Recognition
• Quality methodology/techniques	• Education/training

Figure 9.1. Requirement elements to create and maintain a quality environment (culture).

if possible, customer needs. Mission and vision form the body, the substance, of the work effort, along with goals and objectives (to be discussed in chapter 11). Values surround the entire system and all its functions and activities. Figure 9.3 shares the Citizens Gas and Coke Utility mission, vision, and values statements developed by our executive support team for assimilation by the organization.

Assimilation by the organization is a key phrase. Too often, mission, vision, and value statements end up being no more than just meaningless words on paper because strategies are never developed and implemented to make them the fiber of the organization. Management must accept responsibility for this implementation. It is not something to be left to chance or for others to do. W. Edwards Deming bases his philosophy of management on 14 points that "are the basis for the transformation of American industry."[1] The first of these is to create constancy of purpose toward improvement of product and service. Management is responsible for creating constancy of purpose and making the mission, vision, values, and focus come to life provides the way to do it.

The strategies for doing this begin with ensuring that employees know and understand what the mission, vision, values, and focus are. The communications strategy, therefore, becomes the cornerstone for accomplishing this understanding. I am not, however, referring to just printing and distributing the words. The challenge is to make the words come to life, to make them felt. Part of communications must be the constant reference to and practice of what has been stated. It is indeed walking the talk, practicing what is preached, and actions as well as words.

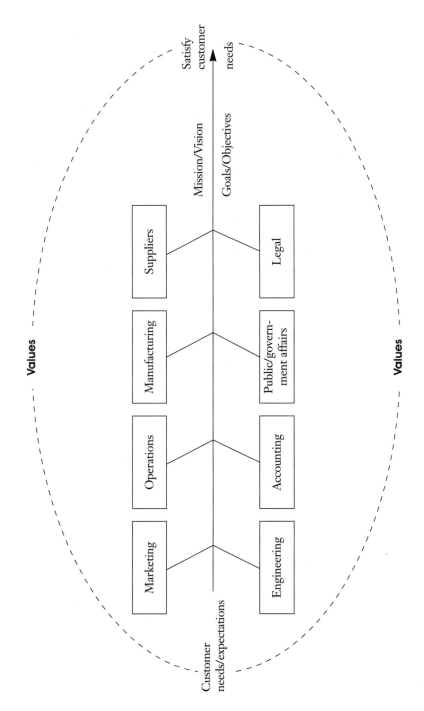

Figure 9.2. The total quality system.

Citizens Gas & Coke Utility
Mission, Vision, and Values

Company Mission:

Our mission is to provide gas service to the inhabitants of Marion County in a manner most beneficial to the community and our customers.

Company Vision:

We will be the best at customer satisfaction in the eyes of our customers.

Company Values:

• We Value the Individual—Meaning each customer and employee should be treated with respect and courtesy.

• We Value Team Effort—Meaning we strive to produce excellent service through open communication, cooperation, and a team spirit.

• We Value Continual Improvement—Meaning we pursue process improvement to assure our outputs, products, and services not only meet but exceed customer needs and expectations. We invest in training and education to improve the ability of each employee to contribute.

• We Value Integrity—Meaning we will conduct our business with openness and honesty.

Figure 9.3. Mission, vision, and values of Citizens Gas and Coke Utility.

I often hear the question, "How can we get buy-in?" The issue isn't of buy-in. It is about management's ability, or lack thereof, to demonstrate the importance and relevancy of what is stated in the organization's mission, vision, values, and focus. Without consistency there will be confusion. Management must be sure its priorities are consistent with the stated direction, that resource allocations reflect the same message as the words, that what is applauded agrees with what is intended, and that consequences support rather than contradict.

Avoiding contradiction is always a challenge for management. It is at the heart of being consistent. We have countless opportunities every day to demonstrate the organization's intent, and too many times we send the wrong message. It would be bad enough if the judgments of us were only in day-to-day increments, but the organization has a very long memory. This is particularly true of how management is viewed, and it partially explains why it takes so long to implement quality and to create a new environment. As we go forward often the reference point for our employees is to our history, both individually and collectively. Management must be sure what it demonstrates is a positive demonstration. It is inevitable, however, that unintended mistakes will occur; old ways and habits will surface. Again, the way in which we communicate becomes paramount. If we face the failure in a forthright manner and discuss it openly, we stand to gain more than was lost. If, however, we hide behind our managerial armor the mistake is compounded.

Another aspect of the communication strategy, one of the early action steps that in its fulfillment helps move the organization toward the quality environment, is the act itself of developing the statements of mission, vision, values, and focus by the executive support team. Development of the statements requires serious thought and in-depth discussion. It requires us to go beyond ourselves and beyond functional boundaries to work as a team for the good of the organization. The agreements reached carry with them an understanding of and an appreciation for what we are about. It makes us ready to start the dialogue with the rest of the organization.

As these early discussions (and sometimes debates) evolve, so too does the realization that another ingredient is required of us if we are to create a quality environment. We must learn, teach, and use a quality methodology and its techniques to ensure consistency of approach and practice. In chapter 3 I described a customer satisfaction methodology and in chapter 4 the issue of commitment and discipline. Only management can cause a methodology to be used or not to be used. Once again managers are the ones most apt not to practice and not to use the necessary tools. Time and again management must avoid complicating the pursuit and must strive to keep the approaches to customer satisfaction, problem solving, and continual improvement easily understood, usable, and used.

Education and training are critical to management creating and maintaining a quality environment. In all that is taught in the organization there must be a common foundation and linkage. Every person must become knowledgeable in what the organization is about, where it wants to go, and how it will get there. From this understanding comes appreciation for the tasks to be performed and the basis from which improvements can occur. Education and training aren't simply for others to do; they are requirements for management as well. At Citizens, we continue to add to our quality curriculum, which now includes courses in basic quality concepts, team leader/facilitator training, continual improvement, measurements, business process improvement, values, and leadership. No course alone does it all. Just as one began formal education with kindergarten and progressed slowly to higher levels of learning, so too must we learn about quality. As in life, the learning never ends and one experience must build on another. Learning requires practice and application of the concepts and methods presented. It too must be seen as a process, one involving both the classroom and the workplace. As we grow and mature, so does the quality environment.

Communication is another critical facet of the environment we create. I have already written a great deal about communication in the context of the conveyance of mission, vision, values, and focus, but there are other dimensions as well for which management is responsible. One of these is about information and its sharing. Once more management's actions or inactions will establish the organizational tone, this time by the manner in which it treats information. The best stated and conveyed purpose and direction will fail to materialize if information is hoarded. Likewise, if functional barriers restrict the flow or need-to-know attitudes prevail, a quality environment will not be achieved. The attitude and practice begins at the top and moves down through management to the organization. In some organizations, however, the grapevine remains the only informational conduit, and these organizations will not know quality.

Another aspect of communication, listening, is dependent on management's conduct. Information doesn't just flow from the top of the organization. It comes from all directions, if permitted and encouraged. In a quality environment, management listens and hears; it receives information and responds to it. In fact a significant part of the quality dynamic comes from freely flowing information, from sharing data and ideas, from working together, from trust and respect.

Trust and respect are among the most difficult elements of a quality environment to achieve, and communication is at the heart of their being. In a traditional organization management can hoard information, use it as an individual power base, and use it as a shield against unwanted questioning. In a quality environment, knowing and understanding are fundamental to progress, and to change. This doesn't necessarily mean liking change, but it does mean making it consistent with the organization's mission, vision, and values. This consistency is dependent on communication, sharing information, and explaining rationale. In a quality environment there is a dialogue about what is happening.

Priorities and expectations are more of management's environmental responsibility to the organization. Just as in everything else we do, we must be sure we don't send conflicting or confusing messages. The greatest opportunity for internalizing the intentions and desires of mission, vision, and values is found in the priorities we establish and the expectations conveyed. Yet this opportunity may instead be disaster because what we practice is not what we intend. The two best examples of this potential are found in the way the organization allocates its resources (budgeting of people, time, and dollars) and the substance of the directions given to our direct reports.

Management must understand that actions do speak louder than words, and it is we, not our people, who most often fail the quality intent. If the customer focus is maintained and used in our decision-making activities, the proper priorities will be established and expectations conveyed. If, however, the focus is on something else, the contradiction begins. Customer-focused planning, budgeting, and human resource management are critical to creating and maintaining a quality environment successfully. Companion to these activities are the performance indicators and the results orientation of the organization as established and conveyed by management.

Performance indicators and results orientation go hand in hand. Once more it is essential that these be consistent with the customer focus and not be mistargeted. The three-phase customer satisfaction methodology provides the mechanics for identifying customer requirement measurements and those of the necessary delivery processes. In a quality environment the process measurements are recognized as being beyond traditional functional boundaries; they are of the total system. The challenge for us in management is to have this broader perspective so that it can then be conveyed to our people. A large part of the issue has to do with identifying the common linkages between organizational, departmental, and individual goals and objectives, and with these the applicable performance indicators and targets. This will be discussed in much greater detail in Part III, but for now understand that what we measure and what indicates successful performance must be in the context of satisfying customer needs. We must not fall prey to productivity standards based on functional efficiency that may have negative impacts on the total system needs. Likewise we must ensure that our pursuits are not for short-term results but remain consistent with the long-term vision.

There is one final element in management's requirement to create and maintain the quality environment: recognition. The other requirements described are proactive initiatives; recognition must be more reactive, or perhaps responsive is the better word. The common driver in all, however, is the customer focus. In this case the customer is internal, our employees, and their recognition needs will vary. It is important to understand that these needs will change as the quality environment evolves. In the beginning management must provide positive reinforcement of team and individual accomplishment consistent with satisfying customer needs. How best to do this should not be left to our own conventional wisdom. We need to let our employees recommend the most appropriate approach. The strategies implemented in the early days will not, however, be those necessary later. Changes also should be guided by the employees, but it is management's opportunity to be appropriately responsive while acknowledging quality achievement.

Before quality our organization had no formal recognition program. In the early years of quality implementation, we used recognition techniques that over time appeared more competitive than collaborative. They conveyed a feeling of winners and losers. As we have matured, we have become more inclusive and less individualized in our recognition approaches. We have become more team oriented. In all its evolution, however, the purpose of recognition has been and is to call attention to and applaud quality acts and accomplishments. Recognition helps the organization celebrate quality progress, and, as important, it helps the organization learn from deed and example.

As said in the beginning of this chapter, there is nothing more important for management to do than to concentrate on creating and maintaining a quality environment. I have to this point shared thoughts about some of the activities necessary to accomplish this, but there are other requirements of us too. As we proceed and think of each of these separately, remember that they are interrelated. They are in themselves processes and subprocesses, but together they comprise the total management system. It is the functioning of this total system that determines how well the needs and expectations of our external customers are met, and of how successful our organizations are.

Note

1. W. Edwards Deming, *Out of the Crisis* (Cambridge, Mass.: Massachusetts Institute of Technology, Center for Advanced Engineering Study, 1986), 23–24.

10 Management and Support of the Quality Process

*The steps toward a quality environment must be
guided and assisted by management. We must have
our hands on the pursuit, but ever so gently.*

In chapter 9 the managerial requirements discussed were primarily about leading and directing, about setting the direction for the organization, and about steering it toward its destination. It was about visible actions and activities. This chapter adds another dimension to management's role, one that until becoming involved in the quality pursuit I didn't know existed. This is about management and support—of management with finesse. It is about activity that, by its nature, must be nearly invisible, a stance rather difficult for most of us in management to assume.

Since others may also find this concept difficult to grasp, it may be beneficial to reflect momentarily on the word *support* before delving into the specific elements of the requirement itself. The *New Webster's Thesaurus* provides a long list of synonyms for the word *support*. I'll provide only a few just to illustrate the attitude and feeling about what is required of us to successfully meet the "management and support of the quality process" requirement. These are presented in Figure 10.1. It's a

• Aid	• Assistance	• Contribution
• Backing	• Comfort	• Encouragement
• Help	• Sustenance	• Bolster
• Defend	• Foster	• Maintain
• Sustain	• Preserve	• Advance

Source: *New Webster's Thesaurus* (New York: Lexicon Publications, 1986), 228.

Figure 10.1. Synonyms for *support*.

great word, one that each of us in management in a quality environment must know, understand, and practice.

It is also important to ensure understanding of the context in which I'm about to write. Remember as we proceed that management and support is not a generic requirement but one tied specifically to the quality process. As the quality journey begins, the dimensions are rather narrowly defined as relating to team activity and their use of the quality methodology and techniques. Later, however, as efforts evolve to everyday teamwork, the quality process will become related to everything in the organization.

In chapter 5 I touched on some of the aspects of the management and support requirement. As I now build on these, it is important to grasp that the intensity of all the managerial requirements I describe varies by managerial level. Those of us at the top of the organization must recognize them in an absolute sense, understanding that they are for us to do or to cause to be done. Although the direct responsibility for initiation lessens for certain elements as viewed for first-line supervisors, there remains a responsibility for implementing the requirement at whatever level. They are requirements for all of management. In each case as I describe the requirement the emphasis is first on the top of the organization, the executive level. It is at this level they must first be acted on before they cascade to other levels.

In the first months of Citizens' quality effort we didn't appreciate how important management's involvement is for successful team activity. We erred in thinking management should be more hands-off rather than hands-on. This is curious to me because we had recognized from the beginning that teams were to be the vehicle for applying the concepts and techniques of quality, yet we left our teams without rudders. We were clearly confused by what we thought we should do to achieve empowerment of the workforce, and, consequently, we confused the organization as well. Even today I struggle with the use of the word in the context of a quality environment because it (empowerment) denotes other than the collaborative, combined efforts required of everyone in the organization, especially management. With these thoughts in mind let us proceed to examine more closely the management requirement for management and support of the quality process.

Figure 10.2 lists the requirement elements. These are described here as they relate to teams, but, as we discuss the related activities, recognize their applicability to the manner by which all managerial conduct is practiced. In their broadest terms they are about directing and guiding tasks, about priorities and expectations, about explaining "Why?", and about communicating.

Cross-functional team support refers to actions required of management to aid and assist teams comprised of individuals from different functions or departments of the organization. Appreciate that time is a precious organizational resource. It must be used for team pursuits of priority needs. As issues are identified either by management or from elsewhere in the organization, the first consideration must be of its relativity or importance to the customer. We in management must be careful not to decide or dismiss too quickly based on our own conventional

---

- Cross-functional team support
- Assign advisors
- Review/approve charters
- Provide tools/techniques
- Analyze status reports
- Recommendations follow-up/ implementation

Figure 10.2. Requirement elements to manage and support the quality process.

wisdom or personal paradigms. The consideration should be collaborative, either before a team is formed or by the team as it follows the six-step problem-solving methodology discussed in chapter 3.

Issue consideration also assists in defining the disciplines and talents required of team members once it has been determined the issue should be pursued. Here again management support is critical in selecting the appropriate personnel, in providing time for them to participate, in caring for the voids their absence will cause, and in being sensitive to the resultive impact on coworkers. The "togetherness" of the quality endeavor is further dramatized through the involvement required of management and the cooperation required of others. Being part of the team has to do not only with those on the teams but with those performing regular tasks. Teamwork involves everyone.

Cross-functional team pursuits often cause challenges for managers with fellow managers. It is not uncommon for there to be peer consensus that an issue needs addressing and that it requires the talents from specific departments or individuals. The impacted supervisor, however, may feel more like having been left holding the bag rather than as a part of the team. This reality must be managed and supported. Team members too may feel like they're between the rock and the hard place because participation usually means extra time, and effort is required to make up for lost time in one's regular assignment or to better prepare for team involvement. Another glaring frailty of the traditional management system is that our compensation practices haven't been designed to recognize such broader responsibilities. Here too we must find new ways to manage and support.

Assign advisors is a seemingly straightforward activity, but management must give careful thought to this action and monitor its intended accomplishment. Figure 10.3 describes the role of the advisor, and from this one can begin to appreciate the importance of this task. The advisor should be someone from senior-level management. The descriptions provided indicate the behind-the-scenes nature of the activity. The advisor ensures that the team understands what it is to do, supports its progress, and provides the informational conduit between the team and the rest of the organization. The advisor should not attend team meetings, but should be aware of team activity through agendas and minutes.

- Establishes team charter, mission, objectives, and time benchmarks
- Advises the team on company policies and procedures
- Guides/counsels team as it progresses
- Communicates information to team members
- Counsels, informs, suggests, and recommends (but does not *dictate*)
- Receives team recommendations and *responds to them in a timely fashion*

Figure 10.3. The advisor's role.

The advisor accepts personal responsibility for ensuring that team recommendations are heard, considered, and a response provided.

Assignment of advisors requires careful consideration of capabilities and chemistry. In the beginning, the assignment activity should be the responsibility of the executive support team or members on it. Later, when the next managerial level has learned about the advisor's role, assignments can come from it as well. Assignment, however, doesn't end our responsibility. We must monitor the advisor's management and support of the team to assure progress is being made.

Some feel that much of what I've described as the advisory role and responsibility should be a separate organizational function. The consequence of that, however, may be that everyone else thinks the responsibility and practice belongs to said function. Quality implementation requires the entire management team to be involved in the process. Many organizations have difficulty because middle or lower management is left out or sees quality as being something unrelated to what management is about. The advisory role and its activities cause management to be directly involved in the pursuit, not only in a supporting way but as contributors.

Reviewing and approving (team) charters is part of the monitoring activity. It is the first formalized act of communicative linkage between the team and the organization. It is done best if it involves more than one person; again collaboration is important. The needed end result is an understandable statement of the aim and purpose of the team. Included also should be a statement from management about the desired time when recommendations should be submitted. More than a simple target for the team, consideration of the submittal expectation causes management to weigh the priority of the chartered issue in the context of other organizational needs. It causes management to establish its commitment to the team and signals this intent to the organization. Reviewing and approving team charters is a managerial responsibility of significant magnitude. Through this activity is reflected management of the human resource as related to the needs of the organization and the time available. We fail to manage and support the process of implementing quality if we aren't intimately involved in reviewing and approving team charters. This is not done for control but to enable us to better manage our resources.

Providing tools and techniques must not be thought of in the traditional way limited by what is required to do the basic job tasks. The quality environment is sophisticated in the abilities of its people, but these abilities must be developed and must evolve over time. The act of providing isn't accomplished by signing a requisition or establishing a standard procedure. It begins with our understanding needs and how best to meet the needs. It requires education and training. It requires practice, practical application, and relevance. It requires management involvement.

The tools and techniques refer to a broader universe than what might be imagined. We must provide an appreciation for combining the talents and ideas of several individuals. We must help the individual participate comfortably in a team setting. We need to demonstrate ways to facilitate communication. We must ensure that there is a process for problem solving and a structure for examining issues and arriving at recommended strategies. We must carefully consider the techniques to be used so we don't confuse or overwhelm. We must progress a step at a time, enabling the individual to build on newly acquired skills.

Management, in pacing the quality journey, must be constantly mindful of the importance of affixing applicability to the tools and techniques to be learned. Tools and techniques of quality should not be taught in the abstract. My previous book illustrates how to link the activity to be performed to the questions to be asked to the tools and techniques to use to gather data for analysis. I still remember being taught statistical process control (SPC) a few years before we started implementing quality. I got very little from the training because it had no apparent relationship to my job. Today I appreciate control charts because I understand their usefulness in continual improvement. Likewise, flowcharting, Pareto analysis, fishbone analysis, storyboarding, why/why analysis, and so on, must demonstrate job relationship to their mechanics.

The applicability and use of quality tools and techniques can best be learned through team activity even though the original exposure may be in a classroom setting. Too often we provide training as a single experience, forgetting that we learn best by doing. We in management must provide the setting where new techniques can be used without seeming to be from a textbook. Team activity can become the vehicle providing this setting. Remember, what we're striving to create and maintain is a work environment where continual improvement is an everyday pursuit, where teamwork is the rule not the exception, and where quality tools and techniques naturally complement our efforts.

Analyzing team status reports is still another supportive requirement. Reading progress reports must be done to glean more than basic information. We must be thinking about what the words say and what they don't say. Is progress being made? Are team needs being conveyed? We must analyze.

"We" refers to everyone on the report distribution listing. In a quality environment, the practice of teamwork recognizes we're all part of the effort, some directly, others indirectly. There is no place for attitudes based in concepts of "it's not my responsibility." Even though we may not be on the reporting team, part of the support required of us is to assist in report analysis, offering advice or assistance whenever needed. Our universe must become the entire organization, our responsibilities related to all it does.

My final task description for the management and support of the process activity is recommending follow-up and implementation. Improvement of processes and their outputs will not occur if management fails to respond to recommendations in a timely fashion.

One of the early teams Citizens chartered was to analyze and revitalize our nearly dormant suggestion system. The brilliant thoughts unlimited (BTU) team was wonderfully successful and in a videotaped skit they delivered a message loud and clear. The skit ends by showing an employee telephoning management and stating, "I turned in a suggestion over three years ago, and I just wondered if anyone had gotten around to looking at it yet." I have shown this videotape to countless managerial audiences, always getting the same instant response of embarrassed laughter.

Management and support demand that we appropriately respond. We must be willing to try new ideas. This is a significant part of our managerial responsibility. It is not something we can delegate or ignore if we are to achieve the quality pursuit. We must also understand that part of responding is communicating. It is necessary that we advise those making recommendations, whether teams or individuals, the status of what they submitted. Often the recommendations will be built on or otherwise modified. If this happens it must be conveyed and explained. We must guard against creating a feeling of failure or lack of accomplishment if recommendations aren't accepted in their totality. We must ensure understanding to encourage rather than discourage future ideas and participation.

We must see all of these tasks as outputs to meet the requirements of our internal customers. They are interrelated parts of a total management system. They have been described mostly in the context of team needs, but they apply to traditional functional pursuits as well. Sometimes the tasks require management in the customary sense, sometimes they require the more subtle supportive exercise. Often successful task completion is transparent, but that is the nature of the activity. It does, however, make it far more difficult to teach or demonstrate to those trying to learn the managerial skills necessary in a quality environment. Those who come to know and understand become uniquely qualified, and the organization having many so qualified achieves unique status.

11 Coordinate and Facilitate the Planning and Resource Allocation Process

In a quality environment there is the opportunity
for management to rethink and redesign
the traditional planning and budgeting activities.

One of the best comparative illustrations of traditional management versus quality management is to share the experience I've had in participating in the evolutionary changes in Citizens' planning and budgeting processes. The changes are so dramatic and the results so beneficial that I will devote another chapter to the mechanics of the planning and resource allocation process in Part III. This chapter, however, will be directed at an overview of the old and the new with specific emphasis on the roles and responsibilities of management.

When I first came to Citizens my initial assignment was to help design our first strategic plan. We studied different planning approaches and agreed that ours would be designed to have goals, objectives, strategies, and action steps. (Each of these are defined in Figure 11.1.) The company had a formal statement of philosophy, but we had not yet heard of mission, vision, and value statements. At the time MBO was in managerial vogue.

Goals	A brief statement of *qualitative* results desired; broad continuing business aims; statements of what is desired to be accomplished, retained, or acquired.
Objectives	The *quantification* of the broad business aim expressed in a goal. They are specific, measurable, and achievable within a specified time frame.
Strategies	The action plans for attaining specific objectives.
Action steps	The specific tactics (actions) necessary to accomplish a strategy.

Figure 11.1. Strategic plan terminology.

Back then, we had a planning committee and a budgeting committee. Planning had a three- to five-year time horizon; budgeting was basically about the next fiscal year. The results of planning were often a wish list of desired intentions, but the real world of what would and could be done was revealed through budgeting. It was not uncommon for us to approve strategies in the planning process only to have them deferred or canceled in budgeting. In both activities, there was absolute, hierarchical managerial control. Approvals were required every step of the way. Control and authority were absolute. Executive management could give or take away. Gamesmanship was a common practice; departmental and individual competition frequent.

In those early days a small group of us would go off into the woods, stare up through the leaves, and dream of great things the rest of the organization needed to do. These were conveyed in the form of goals and objectives, developed from the collective conventional wisdom of these few, often from but a single purpose. In truth, we had two plans: a strategic plan so secret that only a few of us could be trusted with it (we thought), and an operational plan developed and known by upper management of functional units. There was, at best, even in its development, minimal involvement of middle management; there was no involvement of lower ranks.

Budgeting was even more restrictive with even fewer involved. This wasn't so much because of a secretive concept of the undertaking, as it was the view that budgeting was territorial and hierarchical. Budgeting was done by functional component by those in charge. In many ways it was the most absolute expression of power. Within my domain, I would approve or disapprove, grant expenditures or disallow. Needs were often inflated to provide room for negotiation and bargaining. I would go forward to the budget committee as though on a conquest, and my influence was displayed by my ability to bring back to my people the spoils. My departments would compare our budgetary victories with those of other departments and, if mine were greater, so too was my power. The entire process bred winners and losers.

All of this is greatly changed today as a result of our quality evolution. It has happened not because of any specific intent on our part, but as the result of the need for and sharing of information, the effort to explain why things happen, and the need to involve the entire organization. The change didn't occur quickly. It began through the planning process as we began to realize that more than just a few should be involved. But traditional territorial ways were difficult to alter. In our first hesitant step we involved the next level, but had them do their own meeting separate from the executive retreat. We used the same agenda, but the pondering locations were different. We would share minutes from the separate discussions, but these were carefully edited to ensure that no "sensitive" information was exchanged. Over time, we have come to realize that our ability to successfully meet customer requirements, to continually improve, is dependent on involving the entire organization. It requires sharing information and communicating.

Only management, beginning at the top, can cause the change to occur. Although planning and budgeting are routinely recognized as managerial responsibilities, too few of us have thought enough about the way we do these activities—about the mechanics, the process, through which they're performed. In particular, I doubt that we've given enough thought to how these processes and their consequences relate to the entire system that drives organizational conduct. As I reflect on how we once performed these most fundamental managerial acts, I shudder to think of the messages of exclusion we sent to the rest of the organization. Fortunately, we have progressed from those old traditional ways, but even now we're still learning and trying to improve.

We have evolved from separate senior-level retreats to combined discussions, although at first communications were obstructed by titles, hierarchy, and turf. Today even middle managers are part of the process from the beginning, and all levels are encouraged to provide input into strategy development. The plan itself is communicated to all employees, and there is concerted effort to link it with departmental and individual activities. Equally significant is the fact that the two once separate activities are now a single process of planning and resource allocation, combining not only mechanics but needs and responses, limitations and capabilities, and current practices and future approaches. With this has come far more structure in developing and communicating what we do and why we do it.

Having used the word *structure*, permit me to expand on its importance and relationship to management's responsibilities. If some of you are like I once was, the term may seem more negative than positive, but I've come to appreciate how vital it is for an organization to have structure in the way it goes about its pursuit. Too many of us, individually and collectively, bewilder those with whom we work because there is no system or structure to the way we manage. Let me assure you, that I'm not promoting traditional standard procedures, but instead, a disciplined use of customer satisfaction and problem-solving methodologies. I'm promoting better analyzed and defined ways of performing other managerial tasks such as planning, budgeting, and human resource management. Such discipline is recognizable to those around us and provides a sense of assuredness about how we got to where we are and how we are to proceed. Structure is about processes and their relationship to the total system.

Management's attention to the mechanics of the planning and resource allocation processes provides a recognizable structure to what we do. This enables others to join in the effort. Throughout, however, management must provide effective coordination and facilitation. Figure 11.2 lists the managerial requirements for successful accomplishment of this task.

Defining goals and objectives is a very traditional requirement of management, but in a quality environment it entails broader responsibility. Goals must be consistent with and enhance the organization's

```
Goals/objects
Priorities
Budget ($) parameters
Communication to employees
Departmental/individual linkages
```

Figure 11.2. Requirement elements to coordinate/facilitate the planning and resource allocation process.

mission, vision, and values. Objectives must likewise fit within this framework but should be derived from an awareness of process improvement opportunities critical to satisfying customer needs. There is a difference between the old way and the new in managerial technique. Back when we retreated into the woods, objectives were developed from our experiences of things past and perceptions about those future. Truly meaningful objectives, however, must not be developed from conjecture but must be based on knowledge of what needs to improve to better meet customer needs. To those who think focusing on maximizing returns to shareholders is what we in business are about, please reflect on the fact that without customers there will be no interest in investing in our business. Observe the issue of focus discussed in chapter 2. If those of us in management aren't properly focused, it's safe to predict our organizations won't be.

Goals and objectives set the organizational course. They describe what must be achieved to fulfill the mission and vision. They define the targets for which team, departmental, and individual strategies (action plans) must be developed. They provide necessary structure. They don't, however, just happen. They are products of managerial analysis, interpretation, and formulation. If we fail to define them properly, we fail the organization, and we fail to meet our managerial responsibility.

Coupled with establishing the goals and objectives for the organization is the requirement that we properly identify related measurements to indicate how well we are performing. This concept of performance indicators was another evolutionary change in our thinking as the result of the quality pursuit. As we better understood that many of our organization's traditional measurements didn't adequately reflect standards related to whole processes, we tried to determine more accurate descriptors. Many traditional measurements have transpired from our penchant for productivity improvement and the affixing of efficiency standards to work performed. Conceptually, I have no problem with such, but I've come to realize a basic frailty in how these numbers come to be. Simply stated, the fault is that they stem too often from analysis of activities in and of themselves rather than in the broader context of the total process or system. They are too often based on the functional task rather than the cross-functional. Management must determine whether the measurements used are consistent with the organization's mission, vision, goals, and objectives. Not only must they be consistent, but there must be an ability to relate to them departmentally and individually, to link other performance indicators to them.

Performance indicators provide much more than a scorecard of achievement. In the planning and resource allocation process they indicate where the greatest improvement opportunities are. For them to be most helpful, though, it is essential that they be derived from determining customer requirements and related delivery processes. When this is ensured, performance indicators can drive the entire process.

Establishing priorities in the traditional organization is usually a task done by executive management or perhaps solely by the CEO. In a quality environment, many more are involved and management's prime role is to coordinate and facilitate. Priorities should be determined from analysis of performance indicators' improvement opportunities. Once established, consideration must be given to when improvement must and can be done. This determination provides the parameters from which strategies and action plans can be developed. From these come the identification of the most immediate actions and their costs necessary to achieve long-term accomplishment. In essence this is the translation of the strategic (long-range) plan into the tactical (short-range) plan. It merges planning and budgeting.

Management must establish budgeting parameters to provide guidance and to reflect resource availability. The basic tasks of budgeting aren't that different from what has been done traditionally, but the way the quality organization communicates and ponders budgetary issues is dramatically different. By knowing what resources are available and understanding related limitations, management can collectively discuss the organization's strategic needs, improvement time frames, priorities, and resource availability in an interrelated manner. When management does this as a single body rather than as independent competing parts, the organization is better for it, and there is broad understanding of why things are done. The requirement of management is not only to provide the customary budgetary guidance, but to ensure application in the context best for the organization, not as determined by a few but agreed on by the collective body.

When the organization's plan has been developed and resources allocated, management must ensure that it is known by all. We must communicate it to employees. It is *essential* that departments and individuals understand how their functions and tasks relate to and complement the organization's plan. Knowing it provides the answer to why things are done and why resources are spent. Knowing it provides the structure in which programs, projects, and pursuits fit. Knowing it provides the opportunity for everyone to consider how they can best contribute to better satisfy the organization's objectives. Knowing it provides the opportunity for all in the organization to function as a single team.

The traditional organization too often fails to adequately communicate its plan, but, as I've stated before, the failure is that of but one group, of management. Only management can make things different, cause the plan to be communicated, and ensure that it has relevance. Each level of management shares in this responsibility, from the CEO to the line supervisor. Although the way the communication will occur varies by level, the requirement for doing it does not. Management must understand this requirement in the context of part of its job description. We must understand as well that communication of it means much more than just talking about mission, vision, values, goals, objectives, and strategies. It means immersing our direct reports in their content.

This brings us to the final requirement of management in fulfilling its responsibility to coordinate and facilitate the planning and resource allocation process. Ensuring departmental and individual linkages is the managerial task that begins with conventional communication but expands and builds on the first conveyance about the plan to direct reports to involving them in strategy and action plan development and implementation. This task requires us to ponder how our department or function can best contribute, add value, and fit within the total system.

There are many ways to link the plan to departmental and individual efforts. First, we in management must ensure that our outputs satisfy the needs of our internal customers, for in that way we contribute to the ultimate requirement of meeting the needs of the external customer. We must do everything we can to cause our people to strive for continual improvement of processes and tasks. We must ensure that all of us see what we do in the context of its relationship to other processes. Much of this can be accomplished using the customer satisfaction process and its methodology described in chapter 3. In particular, management's attention to the measurements related to customer requirements and their delivery processes can provide substantive and meaningful linkage. From these should also come the measurements, the performance indicators, for the department and its employees that relate to those of the organization.

The organization's plan is the vehicle through which all of this is translated. It provides the framework for identifying broad goals and objectives and departmental or team responses to them in the form of strategies. Within these are the various action steps necessary to implement or satisfy the strategy, and these action steps become department and/or individual objectives. Figure 11.3 depicts this linkage from organization, to departmental, to individual using the planning and resource allocation process. It describes the planning hierarchy from the organization, to the department, to the individual. A separate chapter in Part III is devoted entirely to the process of individual planning, but none of these activities should be orchestrated as separate acts. They are interrelated, and only management can cause them to be done properly.

The importance of the managerial task to effectively coordinate and facilitate the planning and resource allocation process cannot be overstated. I don't believe an organization can successfully implement a quality initiative if this task is not done well. As said before, it provides rationale and structure, and with that meaning and consistency.

Organization's Plan
   Goals
   Objectives
   Strategies
   Action steps
     and resource
     needs

Departmental Plan
   Objectives
   Strategies
   Action steps
     and resource
     needs

Individual Plan
   Objectives
   Strategies
   Action steps
     and resource
     needs

Figure 11.3. Planning linkages.

12 Develop and Implement Policy

Many of us in executive management may think this is not a topic requiring our attention, but it is critically important if the organization is to successfully implement quality. Attention must be given to how we develop and implement policy, to the process we use, and how its outcomes impact the system.

Until the quality experience, I thought the issue of policy was almost sacred in its nature. We at the top determined what policy should be because we knew best, and the rest of the organization should not question its rationale, or should do so very carefully. My understanding has changed, and today I appreciate more fully the delicate substance of what I used to take for granted.

It remains true that only a few of us have the direct responsibility for developing policy, but the way we do it in a quality environment is much different than it was in the traditional environment. It used to be that policy determination was rather singular in its nature, both in who did it and its scope. As the boss, I was in charge of policy formulation, and I usually developed it related to the areas I controlled without enough consideration of the needs of or impacts on others. Although I thought

I was being mindful of the rest of the organization, in truth it was not uncommon for my actions and communications to be lacking. I was not alone in this fact, since this was usual for all of executive management. There were, of course, times when we collectively addressed the policy aspects of issues, but even during these we were protective of our personal territories, giving too little consideration to broader impacts.

Today we have evolved to a different attitude about and appreciation for policy development. We recognize that the organization functions best when we at the top collaborate in policy formulation and give careful consideration to how best to communicate it. We have in fact become a team striving to consider both functional (departmental) and cross-functional policy needs in the context of the needs of the system. In this chapter I will describe important elements of the process for developing and implementing policy. It is essential that management at every level understands the mechanics of this process because we are personally involved in either formulation or deployment. It frames all we do in managing. Its outputs are the products of leadership, management, and support.

In a quality environment management understands that issues of policy must be more than limited responses to immediate needs. In previous chapters most of the managerial actions described require consideration of policy ramifications. The challenge for us is to do the considering before actions are taken rather than after, to be proactive rather than reactive. Equally challenging is the need for involving as many as possible as early as possible in the process, without hindering decision making. This involvement role must be understood by executive management. If utilized it can occur as part of our analysis of an issue and its customer impacts or it can occur in the context of explaining the rationale of the policy. Sometimes this can be as the policy is being developed; other times it cannot. When involvement comes later, questions about exclusion should be expected because this seems to contradict concepts of participative management. The truth is, however, that even in a quality environment, there will be times when policy development is done by one or a few. This requires sensitivity, understanding, and appropriate explanation by those who have been involved, or it will seem like old ways are being practiced. Effective policy development and implementation requires excellent communications as well as proactive, organization-wide consideration and collaboration.

Most managerial actions have policy relationships. Figure 12.1 highlights a few requiring special managerial attention in addition to those described in separate chapters. As the organization grows in quality awareness, it seems the list needing our attention grows at least in equal proportion, which is probably testimony to the latent needs of the traditional organization. If we are to improve in meeting and eventually exceeding customer needs, we in management must accept this fact of quality life. Finding the time will strain the most well-intentioned heart, but the benefits realized outweigh the effort required.

In chapter 2, I discussed the customer focus with customers being internal as well as external. The managerial requirement to maximize the human resource is driven by the needs of the internal customer, our employees, and these needs have tremendous policy impact, often into issues previously not addressed collectively by executive management. Note that I have just referred to customer needs and to unresolved issues. Before describing what we found some of these to be, I'll describe first the process I believe should be used to develop and implement the related policy.

Figures 12.2 and 12.3 show the customer satisfaction process and six-step problem (or issue) resolution process first discussed in chapter 3. These describe the basic methodology or process to follow to develop and implement policy. The steps are applicable whether being applied

---

Human resources

Organization's strategic issues

Improving customer satisfaction

Organization structure

Leadership improvement

Figure 12.1. Requirement elements to develop and implement policy.

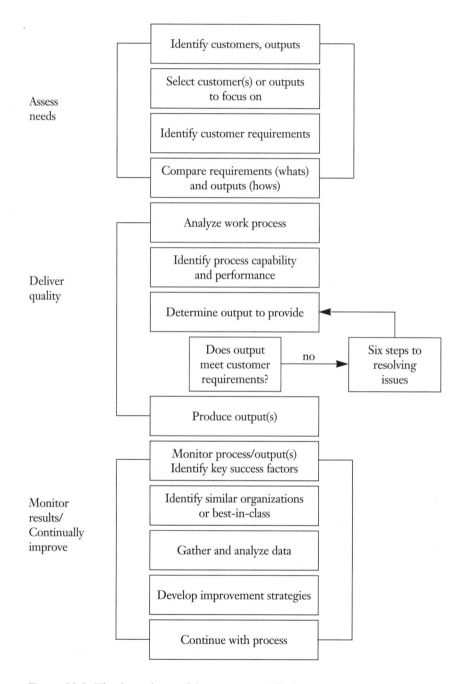

Figure 12.2. The three phases of the customer satisfaction process.

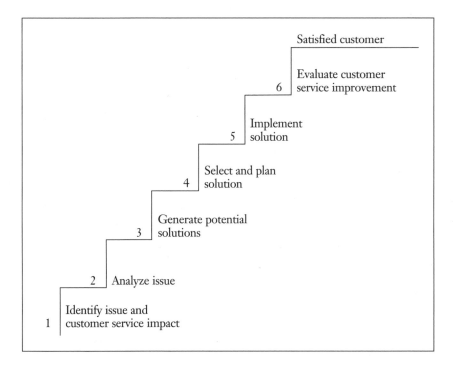

Figure 12.3. Six steps to resolving issues.

by an individual or a team. Since the needs or issues in this case require an output, product, or strategy, called *policy*, the steps are to be followed by executive management. The point of entry into the process steps will vary dependent on when our awareness of the need for a new or revised policy is recognized. If we are early in need identification, we are most apt to be able to use the three-phase process through which we determine the requirements of the policy, then develop the delivery or implementation action plan, and, in phase 3, measure or monitor our success in satisfying the original need. If we are in a more reactive situation, in other words need the policy because of an issue or problem, we would follow the six-step methodology before measuring or monitoring. In either instance, the policy delivery or implementation action plans must have well-developed steps concerning how, when, and to whom communication will be done. To better understand how to apply this to policy development and implementation, refer to this methodology as I proceed in describing examples of needs and issues our executive support team has addressed.

Return now to the managerial requirement to maximize the human resource and remember we used the three-phase customer satisfaction process for addressing needs, including development of necessary related policy. Early in our quality implementation effort, the Citizens' executive support team identified our employees as one of three priority customers. Using focus groups and surveys, we assessed their needs. From this assessment, we learned of five key employee needs requiring our attention and offering improvement opportunities. From these we developed strategies and policies to (1) redesign the employee appraisal system consistent with quality concepts; (2) redesign all compensation practices consistent with the quality approach; (3) provide more personal growth opportunities; (4) encourage decision making be done as near as possible to the point of implementation; and (5) improve the trust in management and the level of openness among all employees.

As in most quality pursuits, progress sometimes seems painfully slow; however, we've already made significant improvements. The employee appraisal system has been replaced by the performance plan and review process (PPR) described in chapter 17. To do this required rethinking the old policy of rating employees. Redesign of the compensation system necessitated modernizing policies about job evaluation parameters, compensation architecture, merit pay, pay grades, line movement, and employee understanding. Employee growth, improved decision making, and trust all required policy changes regarding information and communication. Original needs become compounded as new needs arise from changes made to past practice and policy. This is the dynamic of quality, of the reality of pursuing continual improvement. Although all needs are not yet fully fulfilled, today we are closer to maximizing our human resource by having developed and implemented policy to meet employee needs consistent with a quality environment.

Another requirement of management calling for policy determination is for us to identify the organization's strategic issues. This is a much more traditionally appearing task; however in a quality environment it takes on added proportions. This results from understanding that all activities are interrelated; that their targets are in the context of fulfilling the mission, vision, and goals of the organization, of the single system. Prior to quality we were considering certain strategic issues as we did our annual planning review, but you'll recall that there were only a handful of us involved. Our discussions were based on our personal experience and conventional wisdom. Approaches to improvement were rather helter-skelter, expressed through departmental strategies, limited by their functional parameters. One of the first quality initiatives taken by executive management was to reconsider the organization's goals and objectives in the context of customer needs. Then we formed cross-functional teams with representatives from several different areas to develop improvement strategies to meet applicable strategic objectives. Throughout these early steps policy determination was required (such as who would be involved in planning and how much information to share). We used the previously described methodology to provide structure and guidance. For the organization, as well as ourselves, we expanded our understanding of what the strategic issues actually were; we greatly increased those involved in addressing the issues; and we became much more systematic in our approach. It was the beginning of collaboration and improved communication; the beginning of policy development and implementation consistent with the organization's need for leadership, management, and support.

Policy is required as well to support customer satisfaction improvement. The decision to implement quality is establishing policy. The focus of the effort; the methodology to use; the education and training to provide; the time to commit; the people to involve; the priority of the pursuit; the commitment, the discipline, the leadership, the management, and the support of quality all must have policy. These don't happen without it, and if executive management fails to respond properly, if we continue our old traditional ways, quality implementation will fail.

Some may doubt the failure potential and its impact, so I'll briefly illustrate. I know of one company that said it was going to implement quality and involve everyone to do it. Yet at its first training classes, line employees had to enter by a different door than management. I know of others still having executive parking, executive dining rooms, and other symbols of separation. These are traditional policy subjects, yet we often don't understand the messages they send. Practices of exclusion abound. In information sharing we exclude and restrict. We practice a need-to-know policy; we convey mistrust. Customer satisfaction improvement doesn't occur without supportive policy.

Another policy need of the organization is for us to provide the organization structure consistent with quality. For many this need may take the form of the traditional boxes-upon-boxes organization chart. In chapter 2 I charted a quality environment in both a traditional and non-traditional way. Here, however, I'm talking about structure, not about charts; I'm talking about the form and content of the organization that determines its layers and barriers. Structure and its related policies determine how information flows, how and where decisions are made, and where approvals are required. Structure depicts an open or confined organization. It describes involvements and relationships, and with them career paths and how advancement occurs. Again permit me to illustrate policy aspects of organizational structure in the traditional versus quality way.

Succession planning is a task management must do. In the traditional way, the head of each functional unit (the name in the box) identifies the heirs to that position and their readiness to ascend. This information is passed upward through the organization structure to the top where often a single individual assembles the total succession plan. It is a secret process with no one knowing where he or she has been slotted.

In a quality organization, management matures to an understanding that succession planning is about readiness, but it is more about the individual's developmental needs. It is about identifying strengths and weaknesses, and ways to maintain or improve. It is about objective rather than subjective analysis. It solicits input from others. Succession planning in a quality organization becomes a collaborative effort directed toward what is best for the total system and includes involving the individuals affected. In Part III I'll share our succession planning process and illustrate further policy considerations related to it. For here, though, recognize that the basic policy issues are about the process to use to do it, how the results are to be utilized, and who is to be involved, when, and how.

Throughout this chapter, I've identified numerous must-do policy requirements of management. The most important and difficult of all is the subject of improving leadership. Important because such a small number of us have such influence on the outcome of the quality pursuit. Difficult because it is about us, not someone else. Every chapter of this book describes directly or indirectly opportunities for leadership success or failure. In chapter 14, I'll discuss the topic in depth. For here, though, we are considering the need to develop and implement policy to improve leadership.

First there must be the acknowledgment that leadership needs improvement, then that the improvement begins with each of us in executive management. We need to determine policies around what requires improvement and how to do it. Sometimes it will be a collective (group) need; other times it will be an individual need. The issues impacting the organization will likewise vary, but the executive management team must set the course for itself and all others to follow. The topics will be about process and how we get things done, about information and how we communicate, about people, about how we manage, and about how we support. The topics are about the big picture—the total system. They require that we develop and implement leadership policy consistent with the needs of and as a complement to the total system.

Developing and implementing policy, though a fundamental task of management, is one of the most essential. It should not be left to chance. It must have a process, a methodology. It must have the greatest involvement possible. It requires extraordinary communicative skills. It should not be done piecemeal. It should be done within the context of the organization's mission, vision, and values.

13 Coordinate and Facilitate the Customer Satisfaction and Improvement Pursuit

It is easy to become so involved in all the other requirements of management in a quality environment that we overlook distinct managerial hands-on tasks. We in management also have customers to be satisfied and we must use the quality methodologies to do this. Beyond this, however, is the organization's need for us to coordinate and facilitate all improvement efforts.

In my first book I stated that you need to use the process to further the process. In part, this chapter is about the need for management to use the process—to be directly involved, and to walk the talk. It is about what is required of us to make improvement happen. It is also about the need for us to be dissatisfied with the status quo, to cause the organization to seek change, and to stimulate restlessness for the sake of improvement.

When I speak of using the process, I mean just that. Beginning with executive management, every managerial component of the organization should use the quality improvement methodology previously described in several chapters. As individuals and as heads of functional work areas we should ask, "Who are our customers? What are their requirements?" Having assessed our customer needs we should ensure that our delivery systems produce the outputs to satisfy the needs, and then we should strive to improve our outputs. This is not something important simply because we need to set a good example. It is important because we really do have customers with needs that only we can cause to be satisfied. If we and our organizations are going to be something other than fat, dumb, and happy, we must encourage change. Yet there is danger of pursuing change for change's sake, so the pursuit must be carefully orchestrated. The customer satisfaction process provides the necessary road map.

In this context, some may question the need for change. The need, however, is all around us, and often it is invisible until it is too late. We in management are responsible for keeping our organizations sharp. We are responsible for more than just good reaction time; we must collectively anticipate. Collectively because change today is too fast for a few of us at the top to manage. Look around and see the new products, the new services. Look and see those who weren't here yesterday and those who have disappeared. Consider in your personal life how your supplier expectations have changed and how your choices have expanded. Only management can cause the organization to be more ready, but even then there are no guarantees. The competition around us is dynamic. Customer demands are constantly growing. It is our challenge to enable the organization to survive and, better yet, to prosper. This cannot happen if left to chance. It requires an organization and its management to know what it is about and how to do it best.

Unless we have started the business, most of us find ourselves in organizations that others have managed. There is a history to the way things are done. There are existing policies and procedures. There are long-standing processes for delivering our goods or services. There is the traditional way of doing things. These can be obstacles to change and improvement. To complicate and add to the challenge, the employee makeup of the traditional organization is a mix of young and old. Someone with 35 years in business doesn't find change very comfortable. This is especially true for those in management and is compounded further when the impacts are on personal responsibilities or ways of doing. Yet improvement requires change, and it requires a willingness to make and let it happen. It also requires a way to do it, a process, that is universally consistent. The customer satisfaction process provides this consistency, the structure for accomplishing improvement.

Every level of management, including the executive group, should apply the referenced three-phase process to its activities. Our executive team led by the CEO identified our priority customers as (1) the external customers served by our business, (2) all employees, and (3) the regulatory body governing our rates. Traditionally, these had always been addressed by only functional components of our organization; customers by marketing, employees by human resources, regulators by attorneys and rate managers, and so on. These functional entities still retain direct responsibility, but cross-functional executive involvement using the three-phase process added previously nonexisting dimensions to fulfilling customer needs and improving delivery processes. Throughout the organization, use of the process provided direction and expanded managerial roles and opportunity. It provided the way to coordinate and facilitate the customer satisfaction pursuit and the way to a quality environment.

Management must use the process and by using it the effort goes forward. *Use* must be seen as a direct, hands-on task. It means everyone in management is responsible, not to delegate, but to do. Regardless of one's level of authority the process should be applied in both an individual and a collective manner. In this way the questions "Who are my customers and what are their needs?" and "Who are our customers and what are their needs?" are asked and improvement opportunities addressed.

Beyond the direct use by management it is also necessary that we coordinate and facilitate the application and use of the process by others. One's responsibility does not end with one's self. There is an attitude of cooperation and assistance in a quality environment, and I believe the three-phase process provides the methodology for collaboration. It reminds everyone that the focus is always upon how best to meet customer needs. It enables everyone to pursue improvement the same way. It provides a framework around and a structure for the various quality techniques related to customer assessment, process improvement, measurement, and problem solving. More than a process, it is the means whereby every functional component of the organization can better understand its role in the total system. All of this potential, however, cannot be realized unless management uses the process and helps others use it.

One of the best ways to help others in its use is to ensure that there is frequent reference to it. As the organization matures in its quality pursuit more and more quality techniques are used. These often are complete programs that even a traditional organization could use. The quality organization can achieve optimization, however, if such programs are referenced to the basic process and pursuit. This provides not only the appropriate context for the effort, but it calls attention to other complementing programs and techniques. In many ways it is this associating and compounding that creates the quality environment.

There is also a negative risk. It is easy for the organization to forget the fundamental process, to become so involved in quality techniques or programs that they become the prime focus in and of themselves. Often they bring with them philosophical components that can cause conflicting views and debate. This may be healthy for an academic institution, but it can paralyze a business enterprise. A part of management's coordination and facilitation must be a constant monitoring of the evolution and development of quality, and with it keeping techniques and programs referenced to the basic process and in their appropriate context.

More must be said about this cautionary note. Part of the quality evolution is an ever-expanding involvement of employees. As more and more become involved, and as the environment becomes more participative, concepts, views, and opinions can become more varied. If properly guided, this is healthy. If left to chance, it can cause confusion and damage previous accomplishment. This potential is particularly present among the members of the top two levels of the organization. Executive management must always be mindful that there will be some who may misunderstand, misuse, or abuse their expanded participation. This is not so much their fault as it is ours for not providing the proper guidance. We must be particularly aware of this potential as we educate and train because each new concept or technique can be confused if not presented within the context of the fundamental core of the process.

Coordination and facilitation of the pursuit of customer satisfaction must be part of management's job description in a quality environment. This means we must use the fundamental process and help others use it and/or relate to it. The pursuit of quality can become complicated. It is part of management's responsibility to keep it as simple as possible, to maintain relevancy, and to keep the effort on track.

14 Teach/Coach/Mentor/Develop

Management in a quality environment must assume many roles, but none is more important than that of developer of the human resource. The traditional boss/subordinate relationship disappears. In its place a broader and deeper relationship emerges; one more demanding yet far more meaningful. Only management can make it happen.

Throughout the preceding chapters I have described a wide variety of requirements of management in a quality environment. These should not be viewed as separate independent tasks; they must be seen as integrated components comprising the total job description of management in a quality environment. Together they make up the management system. In their fulfillment they provide dimensions to management's role far beyond that found in a traditional organization.

In the traditional situation management is primarily focused on successfully accomplishing specific functional tasks. Our responsibility was to see to it that the job got done. Our horizons were limited, usually hour to hour, day to day, month to month. Only a few thought of accomplishment quarter to quarter; fewer still of it year to year. We had little, if any, strategic purpose. Our managerial techniques were mostly of directing and controlling; people skills were often lacking. We did little to develop our people to enable them to improve and consequently improve on the way tasks and processes were performed. Training for the most part was something done by someone else or by another department. Through inattention and ignorance we underutilized the human resource. Tasks were done for their moment, and resultant outputs were left vulnerable to change, competition, and others' innovations.

When I first used the customer satisfaction process with my direct reports, I learned that each person needed developmental guidance from me. Later we found this to be a universal need within the organization and we realized that our managerial training was terribly lacking. An assessment of employee needs revealed that the annual individual performance appraisal was poorly conducted, and, in some cases, management didn't even discuss the appraisal with the employee. Fortunately, our early quality training helped us realize more needed to be done than to attribute the fault to individual failure. In fact, the employee appraisal process required redesign, as did management's related role. The outcome of this effort is so significant that I devote an entire chapter to it in Part III. It is a perfect illustration of the difference between management in a quality environment versus the traditional. It also illustrates organizational use of the three-phase process to identify customer needs, design delivery mechanisms (processes) to meet the needs, and measure results for their improvement, all to improve the total operational system of the organization. Such redesign is not a quick fix. It is a strategic positioning of the organization.

The modernizing of the organization, the conversion from a traditional to a quality environment, involves not only process and system redesign, but changes to individual roles and responsibilities. The processes provide the vehicle, but management must know how to guide them and employees must understand how to function within them. Process optimization is determined by the orchestration of all elements. When I wrote my first book, I thought the challenge was to convert managers to leaders. Today I realize that this statement is too simplistic. In a quality environment management must lead, manage, and support.

Our responsibility is not to do one rather than another, but to do what is appropriate. This means we must know and use different managerial styles and techniques as well as when to use them.

The abilities to teach, coach, mentor, and develop are difficult to achieve. They require constant learning and development. There is no other area on which our organization has spent more time, yet has much more still to do. We have spent hours in the classroom studying different aspects of quality management. There has been value to most of what we've learned, and many of us have used tools and techniques from the experience. There is, however, a tremendous amount of behavioral and psychological study to learn from, and most of us in management cannot digest all of it. It is imperative for executive management to determine and implement what best supports the culture and activity desired.

Part of this determination must also include consideration of the delivery mechanism, the process, for applying the theory in ways understandable and usable throughout the organization. Concepts are important, but so too is the structure in which they are presented. Of all I've been exposed to these last several years, I personally believe the concepts and process developed by Ken Blanchard and his colleagues regarding situational leadership best meets the needs of management in a quality environment.*

> A situational approach to managing people is a concept developed by Kenneth Blanchard. It is based on a relationship between (1) the amount of direction and control a leader gives; (2) the amount of support and encouragement a leader provides; and (3) the competence and commitment that a follower exhibits in performing a specific task.

Figure 14.1 presents the model graphically and describes how management should match its leadership style to the development

*Shared with permission from Blanchard Training and Development. It is quoted from the description of the model of Situational Leadership II. *Leadership and the One Minute Manager.* New York: William Morrow, 1985; and Blanchard, Kenneth. SL II A Situational Approach to Managing People. Blanchard Training and Development, 1985.

level of the individual. Of major importance in the concept is that development level is task specific. (I encourage the reader to study in depth Blanchard's concepts.)

In a traditional organization there is little, if any, attention given by management to the need for adaptive managing styles. When considered, adaptation often is based on management's concept of the individual's overall capability to perform, not in a task-by-task orientation but more in a total job description manner. More often the traditional management person may have but one style, and the individual can "like it or

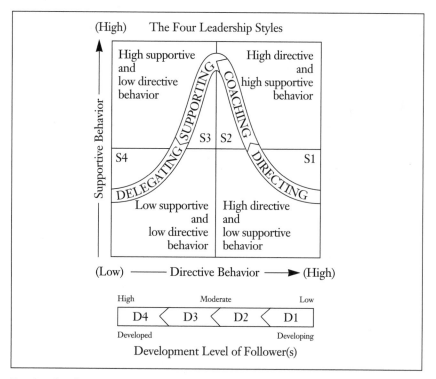

Reprinted with appreciation to and authorization of Kenneth H. Blanchard. Reference: Blanchard, Kenneth, Patricia Zigarmi, and Drea Zigarmi. *Leadership and the One Minute Manager*. New York: William Morrow, 1985, and Kenneth Blanchard. *SLII A Situational Approach to Managing People*. Blanchard Training and Development, 1985.

Figure 14.1. The situational leadership model.

lump it." Until I was introduced to the Blanchard concepts, I had matured in my understanding to the point I recognized the need to have different management styles for different individuals. I hadn't, however, given enough thought to the fact that even the best performer encounters tasks of varying magnitude. Some of these may not have been faced before and consequently require a different managerial response from me. I now appreciate the flexibility I must have in the way I manage. I also appreciate that I must be more in synch with my direct reports. We need to communicate better than we did in the old traditional environment. We must have a more open relationship; must work together; and must frequently and mutually address needs, consider the delivery process to meet the needs, and measure the results for continual improvement. We must use the customer satisfaction process. I must coach, teach, mentor, and develop.

Understanding the concepts of Blanchard's situational leadership, using the customer satisfaction process, and knowing we must coach, teach, mentor, and develop provides significant direction for management in a quality environment. With these there needs to be an additional process for using them, a vehicle to provide structure and a tool to help management and subordinate alike. The performance plan and review process (PPR) previously referred to and now shown in Figure 14.2 can be used to meet these needs.

The PPR methodology was developed because our old traditional individual appraisal system wasn't meeting the needs of our internal customers: our employees. It also wasn't meeting the needs of our organization. We didn't know this until we used the customer satisfaction process. Today the old employee appraisal system is gone and PPR is in its place. Instead of annual judgment after the fact by management of the individual's work product, each of us collaborate with our direct reports to plan and review performance on an ongoing basis. I meet quarterly with my associates to identify, discuss, and plan for specific individual developmental objectives, career goals, and job objectives. We also address critical job performance elements to identify improvement opportunities. Together we develop a performance plan tailored to the individual and linking each person to the pursuits of the organization. Together we agree to how each specific target of the performance plan

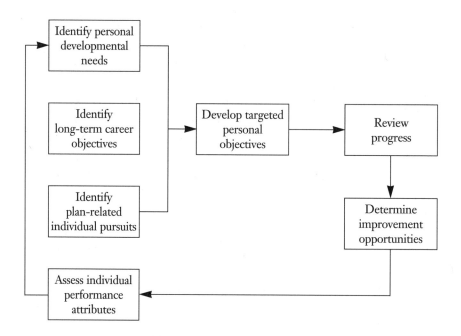

Figure 14.2. The performance plan and review process.

will be measured. Together we monitor progress. Together we agree to accomplishment. There are no surprises.

The PPR is not a report card. It is a planning and development tool. It provides a way to effect continual improvement. It enables me to coach, teach, mentor, and develop in a nonthreatening, nonpunitive manner. It assists me in linking the individual with the organization. It provides a framework for communication and expectation. It reduces stress for the subordinate and management.

The PPR provides the opportunity to illustrate another important fact about management in a quality environment. The processes we use must be evaluated frequently to determine whether they can be improved. For example, although we haven't done it yet, we are considering incorporating Blanchard's situational leadership concepts into our PPR activity to provide the opportunity for discussion of the tasks required to accomplish targeted objectives, the capability of the subordinate to do them, and the appropriate leadership style of the manager. We also are preparing to add emphasis in the PPR to a newly developed statement of organizational values we plan to institutionalize by word, deed, and activity. Another potential change may occur as the result of work being done to fine-tune and link organizational performance indicators to those of the individual. Other changes will occur as we complete the redesign of our compensation system to ensure that it reflects and rewards what is important. A quality environment is constantly changing, and those of us in it must constantly strive to improve the use of the human resource.

The awareness of management's role in the use of the human resource is one of the major contrasts in management in a quality environment versus the traditional. When we begin to practice coaching, teaching, and mentoring, we begin to develop this most important of our resources. We begin to understand what management's job is all about. We help prepare the organization for its tomorrow.

15 Management in a Quality Environment

*In a quality environment management
becomes a system in and of itself. We learn
and grow beyond functional competency.
We lead, manage, and support.*

You've now read my description of what a quality environment is and
what is required of management to create and maintain it. I encourage
you to reread chapter 8 because I believe it will now have added significance and meaning for you. The importance of having a system of management should be apparent, the activities and processes that make it up
better understood. These are interrelated, each is dependent on the
other and complements the other. In this chapter I intend to summarize
what I've shared in hopes that it will provide a succinct statement of
all this book is about. I will also discuss selected managerial outputs—
quality processes—to be detailed in the final part of this book.

A quality environment has a customer focus with customers being
internal as well as external. It has a fundamental core process, a methodology used by all in the organization to meet and exceed customer
needs. Continual improvement of products, services, systems, processes,
and individual capabilities is the accepted norm. Commitment to the

pursuit of improvement and disciplined use of quality techniques create and maintain the quality environment. All employees from the CEO to the line are involved. There is teamwork. The change from old ways to new takes time. The quality environment evolves. A new type of management is required.

In a quality environment management becomes a system made up of functional and cross-functional processes. All that is done is interrelated. Executive management and all members of the management team must lead, manage, and support the pursuit of continual improvement in satisfying customer needs. Management's requirements are to create and maintain a quality environment; manage and support the quality process; coordinate and facilitate the planning and resource allocation process; develop and implement policy; coordinate and facilitate the quality pursuit; and teach, coach, mentor, and develop employees. It is the development of the human resource that assures the strategic position of the organization.

There is little comparison between the management system in a quality environment and that of the traditional. Old ways disappear; new, more challenging, yet more rewarding emerge. Collaboration becomes common; turf attitudes and practices become unacceptable. Through this, the organization's support processes and systems change. A new infrastructure occurs.

Throughout this book, I've presented examples comparing the old, traditional way to the new. There are others as well. Figure 15.1 lists many of the differing comparisons. In each instance there is substance to the issue, meaning it is not only what is done but how it is accomplished. There are processes capturing the mechanics of conducting the required actions. These deserve a summary to permit the reader a collective view of the improvement opportunities within an organization. To those of you who are currently in management, I hope it is a reflective view that causes you to consider when you last analyzed your similar processes to determine how well they meet the needs intended.

The first organizational processes we addressed were those related to the job requirements of management. In particular it is important to understand that one of the major changes from old ways was that we in management collectively analyzed how best to deliver the outputs

Traditional Management (Old)	Quality Management (New)
• Boss/subordinate	• Leader/team member
• Minimal people skills	• Ever-improving people skills
• Underutilizes people	• Develops people
• Decision maker	• Disciplined strategist
• Functional/task oriented	• Cross-functional/system oriented
• Planning/budgeting	• Planning/resource utilization
• Fix what's wrong/results driven (doing things right)	• Process driven (doing right things right)/continual improvement
• Short-time horizon	• Long-time horizon
• Winners/losers	• Winners/winners
• Resource waster	• Reengineering
• Reacts to environment	• Creates environment
• Process-driven measurements	• Customer-driven measurements
• A focus a month	• Customer focused

Figure 15.1. Management styles.

required. We hadn't worked together before to consider what, for example, the mission, vision, and values are or how best to make them more than words. Said another way, we had to first make the management team a team in reality. Although we are better at this than we were, we can still improve further. One of the obstacles to this, however, is old processes and their resultant ways. Even after seven years in the pursuit of quality, there are many more changes required.

The system for human resource utilization abounds with old way versus new improvement opportunities. Numerous processes make up this system, and, undoubtedly, they account for many of the differences between traditional and quality management. In the traditional organization human resource matters are for the most part addressed only by the human resource department. In a quality organization all of management engages in human resource utilization. This is not only about how we deal with people but about the processes causing people to do the things the organization needs done. They are processes of leadership, management, and support.

Some of these processes may not be considered as business processes, I believe they are, and, consequently, they require careful analysis about how they are done. The process of organizational teamwork doesn't just happen; it must be carefully engineered. The process of organizational communication also requires managerial attention. Recognition is another process that shouldn't be left unattended. The process ensuring continual improvement is still another activity we can't ignore. These are all discussed in more detail in my first book, but I mention them here because they are critical processes of a quality organization.

In Part III I describe certain processes and systems of a quality environment. These are not hypothetical examples but actual products of the evolution I have witnessed. All are radically different than those replaced. In many ways, to refer to the old practices as traditional fails to describe them in their actual state. Most organizations' infrastructural processes date years back to when they were designed. They have been patched from time to time, but never redesigned. Traditional organizational processes cannot support the quality pursuit. They should be seen in their true state. They are tired and worn out. They are of another time. They are not of today. They cannot take the organization to the future.

The selected processes are presented in their sequence of evolution. We did not preselect them for improvement. We were required to address them as the result of the quality process itself. The changes came in response to recognizing that the outputs of the processes that existed then did not meet the needs of internal customers, and, consequently, the organization could not improve in satisfying external customer needs.

This brings us to the final point of this summary. The only way the organization can improve in satisfying external customer needs is to improve in satisfying internal customer needs. The customer satisfaction process (see chapter 3) provides the necessary methodology to identify the critical improvement opportunities, the processes of the management system that make the organization function one way or another. I begin in Part III with the processes of planning and budgeting. These are separate activities in the traditional organization and, before quality, were in ours. They evolved into a single process we now call the planning and resource allocation process. In the following chapter, I describe PPR, which took the place of the individual appraisal process. It is followed with sharing our redesigned succession planning process. These are offered to illustrate dramatic departures from the old ways. After these I conclude with a discussion about work-in-progress processes still evolving, illustrating that management in a quality environment is continually improving the processes and systems of the organization. Our work is never done.

Part III:
Processes of a Quality Environment

16   The Planning and Resource Allocation Process

There is nothing more basic to the operation of an organization than the activities of planning and budgeting. In the traditional organization usually they are separate processes. In a quality environment they can become a dynamic single process.

One of the most significant changes in the way our organization operates evolved over the first four years of implementing quality. The evolutionary aspect of the change is important to understand. We did not make in a predetermined way a management decision to combine the two separate processes of planning and budgeting into a single process. The combining occurred as a result of the workings of the three-phase customer satisfaction process. Many times in this book I've said to use the process to further the process, and this operational change is a wonderful illustration of what happens when you do. Even more remarkable is the fact that the redesign of the budgeting and planning processes occurred not as the result of direct application of the three-phase process. It was indirect yet still in its context. The change came from identifying customer needs and analyzing the delivery mechanisms (processes) related to the needs. In this chapter I will share the mechanics of the resultant new process and how we got there.

Although I've previously described some of the changes from the old ways to the new, I'll repeat and expand on them to ensure there is understanding of the magnitude of the transition. As already stated, the old way consisted of two separate processes. Actually, we didn't even refer to them as processes; they were simply planning and budgeting. Except for those who had functional responsibility for conducting the activities, management collectively did not consider the mechanics of how they were done. We would react to specific flaws and fix them, but we never analyzed all the steps and their outputs.

We had a planning committee and a budgeting committee, each consisting of five members who approved, altered, or denied inputs to them. Planning was performed first because it was intended to be long range, but it was not uncommon to have previously approved strategies undergo significant change or elimination when scrutinized later during budgeting. The organization's view in practice was not long range it was short, within the context of the budget. The budget ruled and within its practice we, without realizing it, encouraged competition for the resources of the organization. We bred winners and losers. We created and supported turfdoms. It was not unusual for me to return from the budget review meeting and have my direct reports ask, "How did you do?" The entire process inspired gamesmanship and inflated needs to minimize losses.

Planning was equally flawed. Top management would literally retreat to the woods and dream of achievements to come, of goals and objectives for others to make happen. In the very early days the strategic plan was known by only a few of us. It was top secret and could not be shared. Even as we became more enlightened, we still segregated planning involvements. Executive management had its retreat, the next level had its own retreat. The same agenda but separate meetings. As executive management we still hoarded one of the organization's most precious resources: information. In the traditional organization, information is power and those having it are "the boss."

Even the mechanics of planning were deficient. Broadly stated organization-wide goals were too numerous, often so designed to appease an individual executive's biases. Objectives were conceived from conventional wisdom and/or arbitrary fixations. Measurements of achievement were most often about functional activity, without thought of its relationship to a bigger system. Strategies and action plans developed to respond to how objectives would be achieved were almost totally functional (departmental) responses. (Since planning terminology varies from organization to organization, Figure 16.1 provides definitions for the basic planning terms we used.) The product of the process, our strategic plan, was mostly a collection of operational plans. Even in this regard the process was flawed because some departments used the big plan to reflect their operational targets, others did not. The effort wasn't efficient or effective. In retrospect, it was ugly. Yet we went through the exercise year after year ignorant about how little we were accomplishing.

As previously said, the transformation came within the context of the customer satisfaction process through responding to customer needs. Some of these needs were about people, our internal customers; others were about the needs of the organization and its infrastructure. (Yes, even the organization can be a customer.) The pursuit of implementing quality caused many of the needs to be identified and addressed. In our mission statement we stressed teamwork, and to accomplish it we needed to share information. We needed to work together, not in hierarchical conclaves. The communication process needed to be improved, throughout the organization and, in particular, at the upper levels. We needed a total company understanding of what the organization needed to do and why it was important. We needed to

Goals	Brief statement of *qualitative* results desired; broad continuing business aims; statements of what is desired to be accomplished, retained, or acquired.
Objectives	*Quantification* of the broad business aim expressed in a goal. They are specific, measurable, and achievable within a specified time frame.
Strategies	The action plans for attaining specific objectives.
Action steps	The specific tactics (actions) necessary to accomplish a strategy.

Figure 16.1. Strategic plan terminology.

identify the true critical issues of the organization. We needed to address these strategic issues in a multidepartmental way, in other words cross-functionally, as well as in the customary functional way. We needed to rethink our plan format and planning mechanics. We needed different achievement measurements. We needed to link the organization's plan to departmental plans and to individual actions. We needed to improve plan monitoring and reduce the paper chase.

These improvement opportunities and more became apparent as we progressed in our quality journey. There was, however, one need more important than all the others. The entire planning process needed to be driven by external customer needs, not by conventional wisdom or arbitrary targets or departmental wants. The plan needed to become the vehicle by which customer needs were translated into action plan responses to meet the needs. These responses needed to be weighed one against the other in the context of greatest external customer need. New needs and their strategies needed to be weighed against existing activities to determine greatest value. Planning priorities needed to be compared to operating priorities with greatest customer value always considered. Resource requirements, both dollar and human, needed to be identified and broadly understood. The budgeting activity needed to reflect the priorities established. Budgeting could not be done departmentally until it was first done organizationally. Planning and budgeting needed to be practiced not as separate activities but as one. The planning and resource allocation process needed to become the cornerstone of the management system.

Figure 16.2 shows the planning and resource allocation process and its time frame. Notice it begins with analyzing customer data and ends with the development of individual plans related to the organization's pursuits. From the process are generated the organization's plan and budget. The process is made up of 47 distinct activities, 19 separate inputs or outputs and 13 decision points. (And to think that until quality became pursued we didn't know this!)

The entire process involves employees at every level of the organization. The actual sessions in which customer needs are discussed and goals, objectives, and priorities are established directly involve personnel from three levels of the organization. (We have five and eventually

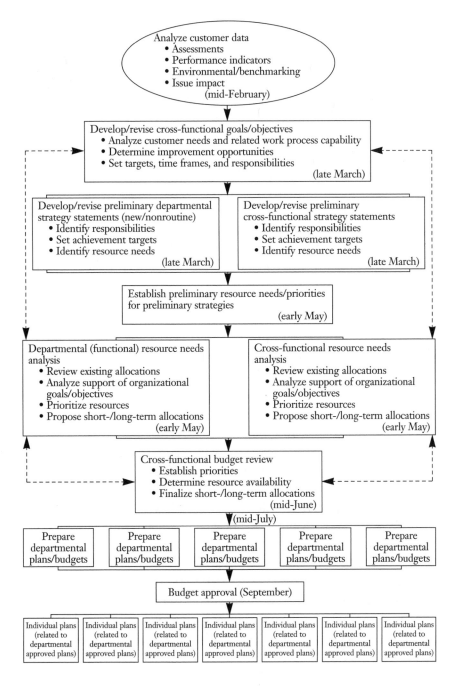

Figure 16.2. Planning and resource allocation process.

would like to reach four.) There is actually no hierarchical limitation to attendance. The only limitation is room size. In fact, in the third year of using the new process, we invited union leadership to join us. Although not all attendees readily participate, and for some the agenda becomes tedious, the entire organization is vastly better informed when the process is completed.

Analyze Customer Data

Until establishing the customer focus for the organization, customer considerations were derived from the conventional wisdom of individuals. Usually these were based in functional (departmental) terms of past practice and policy. For example, marketing had its view, engineering its own view, and operations its own view. Within these there were sometimes conflicting practices and attitudes. Before quality it was often our voices we heard and not the voice of the customer. The new process doesn't restrict individual and departmental inputs; it expands them. As shown, the process begins with analyzing and discussing a variety of customer-based activities from which data are gathered. These include information from customer needs assessments derived from surveys, focus groups, exit interviews, individual contacts, and related statistical analysis. Organizational performance through analysis of benchmarking and monitoring of operational results are also reviewed. Again these are weighed in the context of customer needs. The external environment and its potential customer impacts are also part of the initial deliberations. It is a studious and thought-provoking beginning.

Develop/Revise Cross-Functional Goals/Objectives

At first glance this activity might not seem too different than what transpired before, but, in fact, there has been substantial change. First, and foremost, is that goals and objectives are now based on customer needs. This provides consistency with the organization's focus, mission, vision, and values. A second difference is derived from the number of employees involved in the deliberations. In early quality days we would discuss how best to achieve buy-in. Now we understand that buy-in comes from involvement in the process and from a feeling of ownership as to what is to transpire. There is no better place to begin employee involvement than in understanding customer needs and establishing goals and objectives consistent with them.

Other changes occurred as well. The statement of goals were reduced from a previous rambling of seven to a crisp three. This is important to the organization because they can be remembered by all. Employees need to know the organization's goals because they provide the understanding as to why things are done. Objectives from the old way had arbitrary quantified targets based on what a few of us thought should be attained. Today we are moving toward targets derived from knowledge of where we are as related to where we need to be in the eyes of our customers. I say "moving toward" because we still need to know and understand more about customer needs. In particular, we need to know more about the total systems and, within them, the processes that make up the delivery mechanisms for providing applicable outputs. As we learn about these, work process measurements are expanding from those of functional activity to ones of a cross-functional nature. Someday we'll actually be able to manage by quantified objectives where the quantification is based on cross-functional improvement opportunity focused on customer need. To do this, however, we must analyze all our business processes as they relate to customer needs and expectations.

Part of establishing the goals and objectives is to agree to the time when accomplishment should be expected. This is very important because it frames the later determination as to when resources must be committed. It drives the budgeting decision. Another important element of this phase is to establish agreement as to who will be responsible for coordinating the pursuit of each objective. Sometimes this will continue to be a functional responsibility as in the old days, but as the organization becomes more cross functionally aware, responsibilities assigned will be less likely to match the organization chart.

Strategy Development

In the new process strategy development occurs in two places, the functional areas of the organization and cross-functional teams. In both instances a standard strategy work sheet (Figure 16.3) is used to document action plans developed to attain the predetermined organizational objectives. Strategies describe how we intend to achieve objectives (the

**1994 Strategic Plan
Strategy Work Sheet**

Priority: Date: Status:

Budgeted area no.:   Revised:

Prepared by:

Goal no.:

Goal description:

Objective no.:

Objective description:

Strategy no.:

Strategy description:

Customer impact: Performance indicators: Departments affected:

No.	Action step	Description	Responsibility	Target date	Resources/ needs	Additional dollars

Figure 16.3. Strategic plan strategy work sheet.

"what" we must accomplish) to attain the organizational goals (the "why" of our pursuits). Note that these linkages are indicated on the work sheet to facilitate communication of strategy purpose.

The strategies also indicate customers' affected and related performance indicators that may be impacted. (Performance indicators are previously agreed-on measurements that reflect progress toward attaining goals and their objectives.) For each action step listed, a proposed achievement date is given. The longest of these dates becomes the suggested completion date of the entire strategy. As each strategy is discussed, the group weighs its need and its proposed completion date to decide when in fact it should be completed.

Individual and functional responsibilities for each action step are also identified and agreed on. It is not uncommon in a quality environment for action steps to have multiple sources identified as being responsible for their achievement. This is the documented nature of the teamwork required to accomplish what is to be done. These action step responsibilities also become functional and individual targets that will shape departmental and individual action plans and link them as well to the organization's plan.

Each strategy also reflects the resources (dollar and/or people) required for its accomplishment. Also indicated is whether the resources are new or additional as related to existing budgets. With this information the next fiscal year's budget begins to be compiled. As total resources of new needs are identified, they are weighed against desired strategy completion dates. This enables participants to better understand the balancing that must be done when considering customer needs, response strategies completion dates, and budgetary capability. It also demonstrates clearly the logic in combining the planning and budgeting activities.

Establish Preliminary Resource Needs and Prioritize Strategies

This phase is literally a more timely combination of previously separate planning and budgeting activities. Doing them together has enabled us to complete the annual budget weeks earlier than before as well as to establish realistic strategy completion time lines.

First all participants force rank all submitted strategies to establish their priority. This provides a consensus view of importance. It also reveals where better understandings of strategies are necessary and original presenters can plead the need for reconsideration of a higher priority. We usually rank 100 to 125 strategies submitted in response to 14 objectives designed to satisfy 3 organizational goals. When agreement is reached regarding strategy priorities, we are able to project budgetary impact derived from action step completion dates and their applicable resource requirements.

Existing Resource Needs Analysis

The preceding phase of the process is related to considering new strategies and their resource requirements. The next step is to analyze functional and cross-functional activity currently budgeted to identify and list least value (in meeting customer needs) activities. Resources applicable to the activities are also listed in preparation for the group's consideration of existing versus new needs.

To arrive at the potential give-ups, the budgeting area reviews existing actions as they relate to the recently reexamined organization's goals and objectives. Part of this analysis also includes reflection on allocated resources and time lines to determine whether circumstances have changed. Also identified are current-year budgeted resources that won't be required in the future. What is being sought is currently available resources to offset new needs.

Cross-Functional Budget Review

The final step in the process entails analyzing new plan strategies, their resource requirements and priorities in comparison to those of existing potential give-ups. Customer value is the major determinant of whether new needs and their pursuit outweigh what already exists. This provides the priorities of strategies at this point in time and the resultant new resources required.

The new resource requirement is now weighed against resource availability to determine whether pursuit is possible. In this regard, implementation time frames and applicable resources are once more considered to balance needs, resources, and achievement capability. The result is often adjustment to strategy implementation dates rather than abandoning the entire strategy as once was done.

This completes the planning and resource allocation process. After the steps previously described, final departmental plans and budgets are prepared and the organization's budget is ready to be approved by the board of directors. The old way of planning and budgeting often included last-minute revisions occurring just hours ahead of board presentation. Today the process is completed weeks ahead of presentation day.

Beyond this obvious improvement are several others worth summarizing. All functional components of the organization participate in establishing the strategic direction of the company. All are involved in establishing the goals, objectives, and strategies. All are involved in analyzing resource availability and its allocation. All are involved in establishing priorities and time lines. All are better able to understand and communicate. There is collaboration rather than competition.

With all of these there is one additional significant improvement. It is found in the resultant ability to meaningfully link the organization's plan to that of the department or functional area and it to the individual's plan of action. An organization needs the translating vehicles provided by the plan and budget to describe what needs to be accomplished; how, when, and by whom pursuits are to be undertaken; and how resources will be applied. Individuals likewise need a vehicle by which their personal action plans can be stated and followed. The next chapter describes another process of the quality evolution that provides this capability: the performance plan and review process.

17 The Performance Plan and Review Process

*Nothing is more important to the strategic
direction of the organization than the utilization
and development of its employees. This is not only
an organizational need but it encompasses many
of the most critical employee needs.*

Unlike the planning and resource allocation process described in the previous chapter, the performance plan and review process for all non-bargaining employees was the result of a deliberate process redesign effort. It did not evolve naturally. It did, however, happen as a consequence of executive management using the three-phase customer satisfaction process (CSP). In this regard, it demonstrates how using CSP furthers the quality process. This chapter describes how and why performance plan and review occurred. It also shares the mechanics of the process itself for consideration and adaptation by others considering management in a quality environment.

The beginning of the redesign event occurred as a result of the executive support quality team's use of the CSP. The first phase of it, you'll recall, is to assess customer needs. The team had determined that our employees were our priority internal customers, so we proceeded to identify their most critical needs. In retrospect, we should not have been surprised that heading their needs listing was the topic of improving the process of individual job performance appraisals. The existing method was administered by the human resources department and consisted of a year-end retrospective review of the individual's performance done in conjunction with salary and wage yearly adjustments. A form was filled out using a variety of provided descriptive words and phrases to chronicle the individual's strengths with only implied reference to weaknesses or developmental opportunities. There was no attention given to an improvement plan of action. Beyond filling out the form and sending it to human resources, a standard methodology was nearly nonexistent. Communication with the rated employee varied from none at all to "Here's how I rate you." Even in the best situation it was not a two-way evaluation; the employee listened to the subjective evaluation of the supervisor.

The inadequacies of the old way can best be described through listing the objectives established by the executive support team in chartering a cross-functional team of employees to design a new performance management system. These objectives were derived by having several employee focus groups analyze the issue of the existing nonbargaining employee appraisal activity. (I cannot describe it as a process since it had few consistently followed steps.) The following objectives identify the needs of the employees and of the organization. They also describe the improvement opportunities for management in a quality environment as compared to the traditional organization.

- Provide a mechanism whereby employees and supervisors can establish a mutual understanding of specific job responsibilities and performance expectations.

- Ensure that employees understand the relationship between their contribution and the business plan.

- Encourage open communication between employees and supervisors about performance results achieved.

- Create an environment that enables employees to continually improve their job knowledge, skills, and work processes.

- Ensure that performance evaluations are completed properly and reflect a fair evaluation of an employee's performance so they can be used as a factor in future human resources decisions (that is, compensation, promotion, training, and education).

There is one other dimension to this discussion that is critically important. Achieving the stated objectives are fundamental to the ability of the organization to meet and exceed the needs of the external customers. This is what quality is all about. This is its purpose. There are those who choose to quarrel about the value of giving attention to meeting the needs of internal customers (our employees), but unfortunately they fail to grasp what management is actually about. The human resource and its utilization determines which organizations survive and succeed. We in management are responsible for this determination.

From the efforts of a cross-functional performance management team, facilitated and guided by an outside consultant, came the PPR form described in Figure 17.1 and the process for its use. Another extremely significant aspect of the team's work was its recommendation to the executive support team that all of us who supervise needed instruction in how to use the form and do the process. In addition, the team also recommended that all employees affected by the process be trained as well to understand the mechanics, their role, and to provide

Part I	**Development** (development needs in current job; plans to address; long- and short-term career interests)
Part II	**Performance requirements** (four or five targeted personal objectives for the planning period)
Part III	**Performance factors** (individual performance attributes impacting one's job)
Part IV	**Other activities** (individual pursuits and targets not anticipated at original time of plan development)
Part V	**Overall performance rating** (assessment of overall performance as related to agreed-to plan)

Figure 17.1. The performance plan and review form.

greater consistency in its practice. There was never any such training in the old way.

Many of the differences between the old individual appraisal way and performance management are compared in Figure 17.2. It is important to recognize that the PPR process combines personal developmental goals and job task targets into an individualized action plan. It provides a vehicle for the supervisor and the employee to work together to address career development issues and to set work objectives. It provides a way to communicate with each other about the things important to the employee and to the supervisor. It provides a way to convey and make meaningful the organization's mission, vision, and values. It provides a way to link the organization's business plan to the individual's plan of action.

When I reflect on the way I used to do individual appraisals, I'm bothered by how they were done after the fact. I'm also mindful that when I first assessed the needs of my direct reports I learned they

Individual Appraisal	**Performance Management**
• Annual (if at all) meeting	• Ongoing, continuous process –Planning –Reviewing –Improving
• Supervisor observes, rates, and communicates to employee	• Supervisor and employee work together to achieve mutual understanding
• Broad, standard performance measures	• Dually developed performance measures
• Subjective evaluation	• Objective, dual evaluation targeting improvement opportunities
• No supervisor training	• Employee and supervisor training and follow-up
• Obligatory paperwork focus	• Personal goals focus (development and work action plan)
• No linkage to business plan	• Linked to business plan

Figure 17.2. Differences between old individual appraisal and performance management.

needed me involved in their career development. In both remembrances I realize I lacked a way to be involved with them, and I lacked a method to combine our talents and experiences toward desired ends. We needed a better way to communicate. I have found the PPR form and process a wonderful improvement in the way I manage, the way I lead, and the way I support.

The process starts at the beginning of the fiscal year when the planning and resource allocation process has been completed and the new year's budget has been finalized. Departmental plans in support of the organization's plan have consequently been determined. Individual plans in support of departmental plans can now be formulated. Supervisor and direct report work together to develop the individual's performance plan. The first part of this individual planning activity addresses development and on the PPR form we record the agreed-on developmental needs of the individual. Part of this comes from discussion about the employee's career interests, short- and long-term personal goals, and efforts toward self-improvement. The supervisor adds to the consideration his or her view of developmental needs related to the individual's current job. Usually, I select two or three priority performance factors (to be described in a moment) critical to the individual's ability to do the job. The focus is on continual improvement; the atmosphere is constructive; the effort is proactive. Together we strive to broaden the individual's experiences, qualifications, and skills. Together we agree to the actions we think best will address identified needs (improvement opportunities).

Part II of the PPR form documents performance requirements, identifying the four or five most important personal objectives to be targeted during the PPR time period. (Usually this is one year, but in some instances it may be done quarterly.) First we consider the individual's specific job, focusing on key duties and responsibilities. We reflect on these as they relate to the needs of the individual's customers (those who use the outputs, products, or services). We discuss the activities and the processes that produce the outputs. We discuss job measurements related to the processes. Together we look for improvement opportunities. Together we use the three-phase customer satisfaction process.

Next we address how the individual's job complements the department's budgeted plan of actions. Included in this is establishment of the relationship of the departmental (functional unit) plan to the organization's strategic plan. I strive to identify the objectives departmental strategies have been designed to achieve. (This can be made even more meaningful if the individual has already been involved in developing departmental strategies in response to organizational pursuits.) I strive to make the objectives more meaningful by relating them to the organizational goals and these to our mission and vision. I try to explain why what we are to do is important. I try to connect it to the bigger picture. I teach.

The discussion about the department's plan is directed toward identifying actions or specific projects the individual should target for personal pursuit to help achieve it. Included in these will be team activities in which the individual is involved. We agree to the individual's most important plan-related pursuits for the performance period.

To this point we have selected one or two customer-needs targets and one or two plan-related targets. To these I like to add the most important individual developmental improvement opportunity, providing it equal importance to the others. We now have three to five mutually agreed-on performance requirements or personal objectives. I encourage the individual to develop specific action plans for each of these, identifying the activities necessary for fulfillment and establishing specific targeted accomplishment dates. This provides a basis against which we can review progress. It also provides the opportunity for me to coach the individual in the mechanics of planning, which I believe to be a fundamental job success activity.

Another element important to establishing the individual's performance requirements and plan is to also agree to how I should manage the effort. In chapter 14, I discussed the Blanchard situational leadership approach, and here is one place where it can be used. My direct report and I consider each of the personal action plans and determine whether I should utilize directive, coaching, supporting, or delegating techniques. These are based on the individual's developmental level as related to the tasks to be performed. Before quality there was no consideration on my part regarding how I personally could assist my direct reports in their job pursuits. There was no consideration by me of their needs and how I could best meet them. Today we work together toward achieving targeted objectives.

The third section of the PPR form singles out two performance factors critical to every employee's contribution to the organization. Attendance is highlighted to ensure that the individual understands and follows departmental policies regarding attendance. Safety is also emphasized to encourage each individual to practice and support established safety procedures. Included in this is emphasis on the importance of correcting potentially hazardous situations if and when encountered. We reflect on how these factors apply to and influence the job. We strive to ensure that if improvement is necessary it is known and pursued.

Section III continues with listing 13 additional performance factors as described in Figure 17.3. These were originally established by the performance review team working with the executive support team using recommendations from employee focus groups. Not all factors apply to every individual; consequently, the supervisor and the direct report must

Achieving results through others

Coaching and developing others

Communicating

Continual improvement

Customer satisfaction

Decision making/problem solving

Delegating

Job knowledge

Managing and reviewing performance/providing feedback

Organizing/prioritizing/planning

Performance planning/goal setting

Training/instructing/explaining

Working accurately

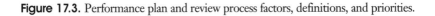

Figure 17.3. Performance plan and review process factors, definitions, and priorities.

consider whether the factor is relative to job performance. When critical factors have been identified, we work together to document how the factor applies to the job and how performance related to the factor can best be measured or monitored. From all the job-related factors identified, I select the one or two most important for the individual's concentration and we come to an agreement on these. They are singled out in the development section (part I) of the PPR. Often one of these is further emphasized with a specific improvement action plan in part II.

The performance factors provide a way for employee and supervisor to discuss critical performance aspects in a constructive manner. If done at all in the old traditional appraisal, the discussion was after the fact. Many supervisors would choose to ignore the activities and relationships the factors represent rather than experience a confrontational situation. The organizational and employee value of performance factor agreement before and during job activity cannot be overstated. Not only is it significant to the development of the individual and his or her ability to contribute, but it is directly related to the entire spirit of continual improvement. It helps the individual to understand that personal improvement as well as process improvement are necessary for the organization to meet and exceed customer expectations.

Section IV of the PPR form is empty in the beginning of the process. It is here that unanticipated activities or projects can be noted during the performance review period. Often these will become section II targeted pursuits taking priority over originally designated objectives. The PPR process is dynamic in its nature. It is ongoing and changes as conditions change. The PPR form is the working document that captures and records the nature of the employee's job.

The process works best in my opinion when performance is reviewed quarterly. It is important that the review is a collaborative engagement of supervisor and direct report. It should include a status updating by the employee of the targeted objectives and joint reflection about performance factors. It is a time when the two work together concerning the employee's job. It is a time when the manager coaches, teaches, and supports as well as becomes aware of each direct report's job status and related needs.

The process never ends since each quarterly review becomes the basis for what is expected in the next. Each year, however, a new PPR form is developed, and prior to that there is a year-end review. At the end of the year the supervisor and direct report evaluate the level of accomplishment of each part II objective and effectiveness in each critical performance factor. Section V of the PPR form records the mutually agreed-on year-end rating of the individual.

Figure 17.4 depicts the four rating choices of the PPR form as used the first three years of the process. It also represents management's difficulty in adapting to new ways, of our adherence to comfortable paradigms. The old appraisal system used single-word descriptors for the individual's performance. *Distinguished, commendable, competent,* and *marginal* were the catch-all terms used to reflect how one had performed. Analysis of managerial practice indicated most used one of the top two categories, with a small number rating employees as competent. Almost no one in the organization was marginal, or, in other words, needed to improve!

This report card rating of employees continues as I write, but we are beginning to change our attitudes about it. We are beginning to appreciate how much each of us—and our direct reports—is influenced by the system in which we work. We are beginning to acknowledge that perhaps Deming's philosophy that employees are either in the system or out of it (high or low) is correct. Most of us in management have a scorecard mentality.

The planning, developmental, improvement, and communicative aspects of the PPR process are invaluable. Likewise there is no question about the merits of quarterly progress reviews. They keep management

---

Exceeds requirements (ER)

Successful in meeting requirements (SMR)

Partially successful in meeting requirements (PSMR)

Does not meet requirements (DNMR)

Figure 17.4. Performance plan and review process ratings.

and employees connected with each other. When this occurs, teamwork is an everyday event. Rating employees destroys the positives of the rest of the process. So why is it done? In most organizations, it is the basis for compensation. In the next chapter, I share the frustrations I have with traditional compensation practices. I have reached a point of appreciation for the influence the compensation system has on the organization, but as yet I haven't found the one that is unquestionably correct for management in a quality environment.

Perhaps, however, it is appropriate to call attention to what remains to be improved. Quality is about continual improvement of products and services, of systems and processes, of individuals, of management, and of the organization. Quality, itself a process, never ends; it is always evolving. It is change. It cannot be left to chance. We who are management must lead, manage, and support the evolution.

18   The Compensation System

*The organization's compensation system is
comprised of much more than salaries, wages,
and benefits paid. It is the translator of all the
organization is about. It communicates what has
value and worth. Its composition is of multiple
processes and elements. It is extremely complex
and difficult to correctly design. In a quality
environment it must support the effort.*

As I confessed in the previous chapter, this topic is still in the design
stage. A tremendous amount of issues identification and analysis has
occurred over more than five years of trying to correctly respond to the
inadequacies of the old methods. We are making progress toward
redesign of the old system, but we are well aware that some of what we
change will need further alteration. This chapter will share what we've
learned and what is still unknown. Perhaps it can provide some shortcuts
for others. Certainly, in the least, it should describe deficiencies in traditional compensation and related practices. It should also dramatize the
importance of in-depth analysis before implementing improvement
strategies.

One of the reasons it has taken us so long to get to where we are is that we have spent time designing and implementing inappropriate processes. Some say quality is doing the right thing the right way the first time. What I am about to describe should provide ample evidence to the importance of ensuring you're in fact doing the right thing. It also illustrates the risks present in process redesign even in the best of circumstances, even in pursuit of quality, even in trying to satisfy customer needs.

As an organization strives to improve its core systems and processes, it must maintain constant and consistent relevancy to their impact on external customers. Management must be mindful of pursuits intended to meet internal customers' needs which may not have had broad enough consideration. Where we are today began from the results of the executive support team's first assessment of employee needs and our use of the customer satisfaction process. We identified specific needs, analyzed and redesigned the processes related to them, and, in measuring for continual improvement, eventually realized the needs were more complex than first thought. Today we understand that the compensation system must satisfy both employee and organizational needs in the context of how they can better serve the external customer.

The originally identified employee need was to provide pay for performance. At the time, only executive management had an incentive plan. Management thought the employee message was to broaden incentive opportunities and we initiated efforts to design incentive pay programs. The result was a confusing mix of an expanded management incentive plan, profit sharing, and gain sharing. The word *confusing* is important to understand because it accurately describes the employee impact of our well-intentioned efforts. The programs didn't communicate quality objectives. Rather than encouraging teamwork and collaboration they supported competition. Not all employees were covered by the same plan. Targets varied. The external customer focus was blurred. Adding to the communicative confusion was executive management's persistence that the appraisal system redesign should tie compensation to an appraisal score. We simply didn't understand the actual needs; consequently, the processes altered or installed didn't produce the required product.

When the follow-up employee needs assessment revealed that pay for performance was still a critical improvement opportunity, executive management began to appreciate more fully the complexities of the compensation system. We began to understand there was more to the issue than measuring or in some way determining performance and rewards. Fortunately, our quality journey was further along. We had evolved to a higher level of organizational awareness. We had improved since first faced with the challenge.

Today we are progressing toward a redesigned compensation system. I can't yet describe all facets and processes of it, but there are several components worthy of discussion. We know the new system must focus the employee on our mission, "to satisfy the needs of our customers" and our vision "to be the best in satisfying customer needs in the eyes of our customers." It must support and be consistent with the values of the organization as described in Figure 18.1. We have identified human resource practices and parameters for each of the organizational values the system must reflect. These are described in the following paragraphs.

We value the individual.

- Individual contribution will be recognized.

- People add value through the work they perform and their individual skills and behaviors.

We value the individual. Each customer and employee should be treated with respect and courtesy.

We value team effort. We strive to produce excellent service through open communication, cooperation, and a team spirit.

We value continual improvement. We pursue process improvement to ensure our outputs, products, and services not only meet but exceed customer needs and expectations. We invest in training and education to improve the ability of each employee to contribute.

We value integrity. We will conduct our business with openness and honesty.

Figure 18.1. Company values.

- Self-management and empowerment with responsibility will be encouraged.

- Equitable treatment, not necessarily the same treatment, will be supported.

- The need for a diverse work force will be recognized in hiring and promotional policies.

We value teamwork.

- Each person depends on others for his or her success.

- Compensation will be based, in part, on team and total system performance/results.

- We will promote from within when possible.

- We expect teamwork and will provide the information to facilitate it.

We value continuous improvement.

- We expect job descriptions and individuals to change.

- We will provide opportunities to enhance skills.

- We expect individuals to learn new skills.

We value integrity.

- We expect clear conveyance of expectations and feedback about performance.

- We expect frequent, honest feedback from supervisors, subordinates, and peers.

- We strive to provide a safe work environment.

We have considered the purpose of compensation as applicable to our organization and have agreed that compensation practices must

- Reflect the value the individual provides to the company and to the organizational unit

- Support the concept of one company focused on customer service and value

- Recognize enhanced performance and professional development
- Encourage and reinforce collaborative behavior
- Emphasize performing tasks that add value to the customer, rather than simply doing a job

From these basic but general parameters more specific ones were established using team analysis, focus groups, and open discussion. Just as in the redesign of the old appraisal system into the performance plan and review process, broad employee involvement has enhanced the effort to redesign the compensation system. Management and direct reports have collaborated and communicated moving the organizational understanding of system intent and purpose to improved levels. The more specific parameters state that compensation

- Must clearly link to and support the organization's mission, vision, values, and strategic plan.
- Must link to and support PPR performance factors
- Must encourage the focus on the external customer
- Will be based on a combination of individual, group, and organizational performance factors
- Will recognize the value of acquiring new skills and competencies
- Will be above average but not the highest in market position for base compensation
- Will define internal equity as the value of a position based on organizational criteria (In establishing value, consideration will be given to relevant competencies, skills, knowledge, behavioral requirements, organizational impacts, and working conditions.)
- Will consider the unique contributions of each incumbent

At this point, it is believed that the completed compensation system will have three components: (1) base compensation, (2) merit pay, and (3) incentive pay. Further analysis is required about each to determine which of several optional approaches best meet the design parameters. Base compensation issues have caused us to acknowledge we must also redesign the organization's job evaluation process, which has been used for over 30 years. The way the organizational value of new and revised jobs is determined is critical to the quality of the compensation system. If the elements aren't consistent with the organizational value system, the values become mere words rather than reflected practice. Likewise, the job evaluation process must support the organization's strategies regarding quality and customer service. Job evaluation and base compensation are the cornerstones for the development and implementation of a compensation system supporting a quality environment.

The new job evaluation process will be one designed by management and employees working together. Base compensation, merit pay, and incentive pay determinations will also be derived through collaboration. The effort in itself will be a significant improvement when compared to the old, traditional methods. In the old, for example, there has never been any attempt to educate employees about how job value is determined. Even most of management doesn't understand the process or its components. Those who do understand protect their knowledge for it puts them ahead of their counterparts. Just as in the old budgeting process, the old job evaluation process encouraged gamesmanship. They produced winners and losers. They supported turf building, not quality.

The compensation system and its processes are integral parts of the organization's infrastructure. Management must understand their components and practices. To ignore or leave to a few is almost certain to assure inconsistency and abuse. To attempt to modernize managerial philosophy and conduct without redesigning fundamental business systems severely limits successful quality implementation. Nothing is more fundamental to the organization than its compensation practices. Salaries or wages impact every employee. They communicate job and individual worth. They reflect priorities. They convey what is important. They support or conflict with quality.

This discussion provides the opportunity to further illustrate a previously described quality fundamental. Figures 18.2 and 18.3 show the customer satisfaction process and six-step issue resolution processes. I have stated and now restate, "Use the process to further the process." It is this methodology to which I refer. Redesign of the compensation system originated with the executive support team using the process phase by phase. In the second—process—phase we thought we had successfully addressed customer needs and outputs (pay for performance

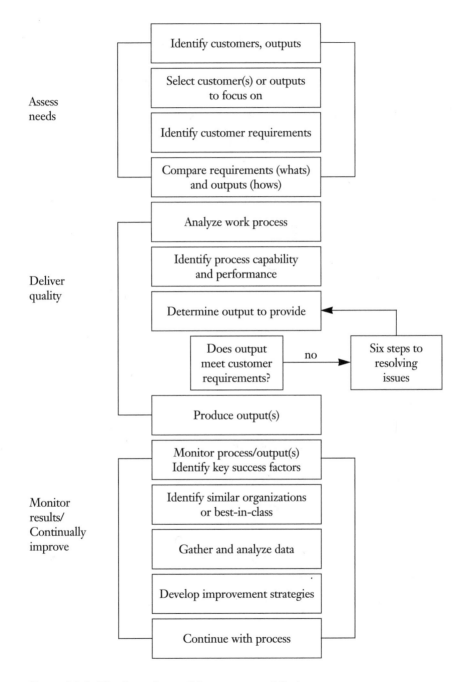

Figure 18.2. The three phases of the customer satisfaction process.

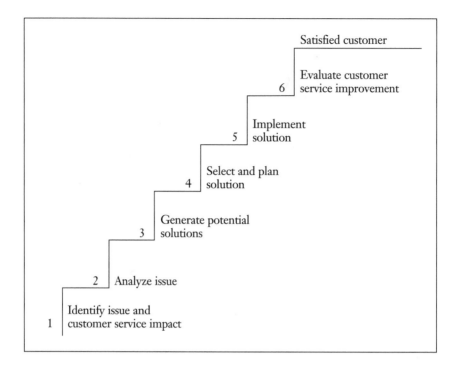

Figure 18.3. Six steps to resolving issues.

programs) were produced (implemented). When we did the third phase, measurement, we learned we had improvement opportunities and needed to use the six-step methodology to implement new, improved strategies. The cycle is continuous. It never ends. Management must always ask whether needs are being met and whether processes can or should be improved. It is the way organizations improve products and services. It is the way organizations evolve to levels of success beyond competition's reach. The zenith is made possible because only a few successfully combine focus, methodology, processes, policy, and practice. Only a few know how to manage for a quality environment.

19 Quality Policies and Practices

Focus, methodology, and processes are not the only elements of the management system in a quality environment. Policies and practices of management also are critical to leadership, management, and support.

The organization's policies and practices have major influence on the level of quality implementation attained. In the traditional organization, policies and procedures have accrued over years and years of managerial dictate. Few of us in management, if any, have read all that those who have preceded us have stated. Our employees are more apt to know the rules than we are. Certainly, they know when and how to bend them. It is also certain they know which ones hinder sensible operation.

In a quality environment, management must analyze existing policies and procedures to determine their consistency and relevancy to the quality initiative. They cannot send contradictory messages. What, for example, do policies and procedures communicate about authority and responsibility? How many levels and steps are in the approval process? Management cannot espouse empowerment on the one hand and yet leave in place rules that say "Thou shalt not act without permission." An employee can be fired for breaking a rule, therefore rules cannot be of old mandates. Analysis will find many improvement opportunities in the organization's policies and procedures. Adequate analysis necessitates employees and management reviewing practices together. The customer focus provides a common framework for the effort.

The evolution of the quality initiative will cause some policies and procedures to be scrapped and others to be revised. Using the process to further the process forces management to examine its operational apparatus. There will, however, be new needs identified, needs for which policy doesn't exist. These will cause management to probe deeply into its conscience, to debate its psychology and philosophy. As this occurs time and again, management progresses in the ability to lead, manage, and support. As management progresses, the organization progresses. This is continual improvement in practice.

When traditional-management executives think of continual improvement it is about process and/or productivity improvement. When employees think of these they think of job insecurity. As we moved from easy opportunities to improve in meeting customer needs to those more challenging, we realized we needed to address the issue of job security. Substantive process improvement could not occur until the needs of employees and the organization were considered together. We had evolved to an understanding that process improvement required the involvement of those in the process—those doing the tasks. Adjacent to this understanding was the appreciation that it isn't realistic for management to expect employees to design themselves or friends or coworkers out of a job.

A policy to address these newly realized needs didn't exist; business process improvement paused while the issues were analyzed and practices determined. The result is shared in its entirety in Appendix A, but the features of the displacement policy attempt to strike a balance between employee and organizational needs. It attempts to be fair. It is a two-sided statement acknowledging responsibilities of the organization to the individual and the individual to the organization.

The policy is written in the context that employees will be displaced due to changes in manning needs or reorganization. (The traditional organization often fails to acknowledge openly that this is a business reality.)

In its preamble, management states its intent to minimize the employee impact of manning changes to the extent practical. We state our desire to retain employees providing they have the skills to perform other tasks. We recognize that outplacement may, however, be necessary, but we state our intent to assist the employee in finding other employment.

In the statement, procedural steps are outlined describing actions and responsibilities. The first step requires the reorganizing department to develop a plan describing what is to take place and providing a timetable for accomplishment. The plan provides approach awareness capability for not only the affected employees but for all the organization. As fundamental as the plan is to minimizing manning change impact, there is one need even more basic. Management must communicate the intended change and its rationale. This communication must be to the employees directly and indirectly involved. It must go beyond the affected department and be shared with the organization. It is done this way in a quality organization. In the traditional organization, however, events of this nature are left to the grapevine to announce and interpret.

Another feature of the displacement policy is early notification of anticipated manning adjustment. Note the difference between the quality approach and the traditional approach. In the traditional, there often is no advance notification, even though management is aware changes are pending. The irony of the old way is that usually the pending event is not secret at all, and the grapevine is once again the informational conduit rather than management. It is no wonder that employees become distrusting and fearful of change. The unfortunate aspect of it is that management misses a wonderful opportunity to make the organization more receptive to and understanding of change. Management creates a resistance to continual improvement. Management fails to lead, manage, and support.

The policy tries to make the future less uncertain. Its intent is to convey that there is still opportunity during and after change. Affected employees are given the opportunity to be selected for remaining jobs in the department. If not successfully placed there, time is provided to find jobs elsewhere in the organization. Skills improvement training is offered. Counseling is provided. Salary and benefits are kept stable during a six-month search period. A 24-month differential payment is offered if the employee chooses a new job at a lower pay grade. Finally, if all else fails, severance pay and outplacement counseling are provided. Quality management tries to understand and meet employee needs. Quality management tries to be fair. Some who are schooled in traditional management may think fairness is too soft an attribute for the successful organization. For those swayed in this direction, I remind you that the business objective at the center of the employee displacement issue is to enhance organizational pursuit of continual improvement.

Continual improvement cannot occur without information sharing and communication. It cannot occur with a management versus employee, employee versus management mind-set. Collaboration is essential. Organizations do not succeed when employees are expendable. The challenge is to achieve win/win improvement. It is management's responsibility and opportunity to orchestrate.

As quality implementation proceeds, management will find numerous such improvement opportunities in the way managing is done. Another example that further illustrates the differences between the traditional and quality management techniques is in the practice of succession planning. Before quality, organization replacement charts were developed annually by the management of each functional unit. The manager of the unit would draw an organization chart showing his or her position and its direct reports. In each box would be named the incumbent and one or two replacements as determined by the manager. Performance of each was coded. The readiness of heirs to the positions was also coded. It was a secret process that, when charted, was passed up through the chain of command. Each higher managerial authority developed his or her own direct report replacement chart until, finally, the vice presidents did theirs. Each of these was submitted to the president. There was no discussion about the separate reports.

The organizational inadequacy of the old process didn't end there, however. The president prepared a replacement chart and shared it with the board of directors. It too was secret. Even as executive vice president I never saw it. The process described isn't just about organization replacement charts. It is about the management system in its entirety: old versus new. It is about where and how decisions are made. It is about hierarchy. It is about information sharing and communication. It is about involvement and the lack of involvement. It is about the environment we in management create through policy and practice.

Today succession planning is done differently. The process is redesigned, yet we didn't just one day decide to do so. The change came naturally as part of the quality evolution. As we in management became more aware of our responsibilities regarding human resource utilization, we began to appreciate more fully the opportunities present in developing employees. We began to understand we needed to better utilize the management team. We needed to rethink our own processes and practices.

Succession planning in a quality environment should be an open, collaborative process. Today replacement charts are developed in consultation with each other. We are careful to emphasize that they reflect what is at this moment, not necessarily what is in the distant future. The process begins with each direct report suggesting his or her replacement in the context of "If I should win the lottery today, I would recommend. . . ." The manager and the direct reports discuss the recommendations, including the manager's own replacement. Incumbent needs for each job are discussed and replacement recommendations are weighed. Much more than functional or task skills are considered. For example, Figure 19.1 lists the characteristics and attributes agreed to by the executive support team (the president and vice presidents) as necessary in being a team member. These were used for benchmark analysis of possible replacements. Consensus is sought regarding each individual considered. Strengths and improvement needs are identified and noted. The effort is a blend of fact and opinion, but the group discussion keeps it focused on objectivity.

Much more than the organization's replacement chart comes from the process. Traditional functional considerations are broadened beyond usual organizational lines. Lateral opportunities are identified as are consolidation potentials. Most valuable, however, is the tool it provides management in working with its direct reports. Succession planning outcomes are discussed openly with each, but only as they relate to each individually. Knowing it is a consensus view makes the assessment much more palatable. The individual's strengths and improvement opportunities are considered together. I strive to move the discussion of improvement needs from a retrospective to a futuristic view. The discussion is about a snapshot

Versatility—ability to communicate in different ways to be certain that a theme/position/thought is both sent and received

Interest in the role—desire and willingness to do all the things required

Contribution to the team—interest of the team comes before that of the individual

Good communicator—good listener

Good at collaboration/teamwork/diplomacy

Capacity to learn—intellectual capacity

Trust—able to earn trust

Maturity/seasoning

Humility

Compassion for others

Global view

Commitment

Not competitive

Not cynical

Figure 19.1. Executive support team characteristics and attributes.

in time, not about forever. My direct report and I have before us the basis from which we can develop improvement strategies. We can discuss career opportunities objectively. The conclusions we reach are translated and documented into the individual's PPR plan. Succession planning becomes part of the continual improvement process.

The examples of the displacement policy and succession planning are provided as more than techniques one might consider. They are meant to demonstrate how important it is for management to examine its own house. Old policies and practices cannot be ignored for they have the potential of being obstacles in the way of the quality journey. It is, however, important to emphasize that the best analysis and redesign will occur as part of the natural evolution of the quality environment. A state of readiness must first be reached and in many ways management readiness takes longest to achieve.

20 The Line of Sight Process

Line of sight: A method of linking activities and measurements to enable employees and/or teams (using the customer satisfaction process) to better understand how the task (process) they perform contributes to the organization's mission, vision, values, and goals. It also provides the rationale for continual improvement and links the individual's PPR process to the organization's strategic plan.

I have only recently been introduced to the line of sight concept, but I enthusiastically applaud it. The term is derived from the name taken by a cross-functional team, the line of sight team (LOST). (Quality teams can and should have a sense of humor. It makes improvement fun.) The team's charter was to find ways for the organization and the employees in it to see and appreciate the purpose and system of what is done. The team members were to show how to link organizational pursuits to functional and individual pursuits. They were to find a method to help us identify improvement opportunities of the greatest importance. They decided all of this meant they were to keep the organization from becoming lost.

This chapter is more than simply a recounting of the outcomes of the LOST team. It is also intended to emphasize the importance of understanding the interrelationships of all this book is about. The reader must conceptually formulate chapter after chapter into a connected series of related organizational processes, policies, and practices. When activated together their outcome is a quality environment. If seen this way, they provide a line of sight for management. They provide a management system.

An organization in the pursuit of quality will generate a tremendous number of previously unrealized needs for which improvement initiatives should be considered. Without a way to prioritize these, effort can be misdirected and time wasted. An organization can rather easily become confused if management allows well-intended energies to be spent on improvements of less customer value than others. Line of sight is about prioritizing. It provides a process for identifying what is most important to do.

There are three fundamental quality processes that the line of sight process connects, the customer satisfaction process (chapter 3), the planning and resource allocation process (chapter 16), and the performance, plan and review process (chapter 17). From the customer satisfaction process comes the improvement strategies that are considered in the planning and budgeting (resource allocation) activities. From the planning and resource allocation process comes what functional units and individuals are to pursue. These identified pursuits are intended to accomplish objectives critical to meet customer needs successfully. A weakness can exist in the improvement system, however, if the objectives have not been properly founded. Key to appropriate objective setting is understanding where meaningful differences exist between customer expectations and the organization's output. Measurements become the fundamental business driver, but they must be of the correct things. They must be derived from the key business processes necessary to meet and exceed customer requirement.

These fundamental or core business processes are difficult to analyze because they comprise activities of several different functional components. Adding to the analyses challenge is the fact that those who know the tasks of each applicable job are those actually doing the work, not management. Successful business process analysis must therefore include all involved units and all involved persons. It takes a special culture to do business process analysis. It takes an even more advanced culture to truly improve business processes. It takes a quality environment and a quality organization.

In the three-phase customer satisfaction process, performance measurement as related to customer requirements is the final part of the first phase. In the second phase, delivery, measurements related to the work process applicable to the customer requirement are identified. The question "Does the output meet the customer requirement?" actually compares the business process to the customer need. The comparative basis in each case is determined by the measurements from each phase. A linkage capability exists.

Remember from my earlier statement that the challenge is one about priorities; otherwise, there are more needs and more improvement opportunities than the organization can address. What is most important to the customer determines where improvement effort should be directed. Only in-depth analyses can provide the data necessary to compare key business process outputs to key customer requirements. One must know the customer and the organization's processes. Perhaps this is what Deming is trying to tell us when he urges we acquire "profound knowledge." Prioritized improvement opportunities determined in the manner described crystallize what the organization's objectives should be. I now appreciate what MBO intended and see the day sometime soon when the objectives in our strategic plan will have been developed through analysis of priority customer needs compared to process capability. When objectives are developed in this manner and the organization's priorities are targeted, the strategies or action plans developed for their attainment are made meaningful to those engaged in their accomplishment.

Figure 20.1 modifies the basic CSP diagram to illustrate that priority process improvement fits naturally into the basic concepts of quality first described. The shaded areas of the diagram are those added to the original and depict the prioritizing steps just discussed. The linkage of high-level priority customer needs to high-level processes that produce the required outputs is the first step in the line of sight process. What follows is a step-by-step analysis of each process and the activities and tasks within it. These are flowcharted and diagrammed. For each,

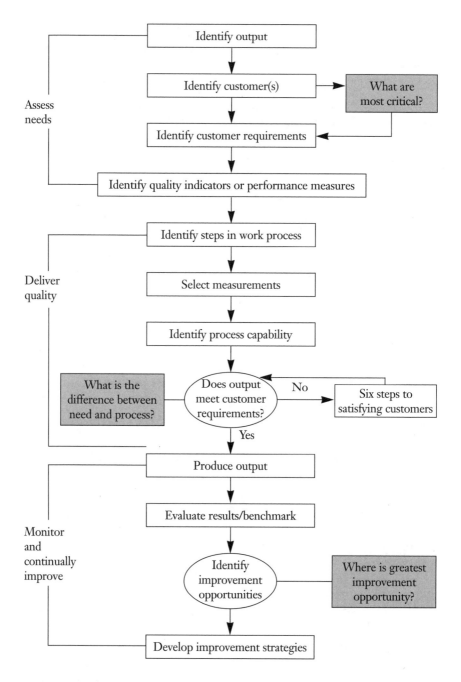

Figure 20.1. Flowchart of customer satisfaction process.

measurements of the activity and task are identified. Control charts of the measurements are maintained to analyze variability and determine where improvement opportunities exist. The improvement opportunities become targeted priority objectives in the organization's strategic plan.

The high-level linkages and measurements of customer needs and related processes can now be translated easily to functional work units and employees. In an earlier chapter I discussed the importance of management explaining "Why?" Line of sight provides the rationale and lets employees see what needs to improve. It explains "Why?" and if done correctly involves the employee in the development of the explanation. Priorities reflected with applicable measurements remain critical through each step of process, activity, and task analysis. As was done for the organization, targeted priority improvement opportunities become work unit objectives. The action plans developed in response to these become task improvement objectives for the individual employee. These are translated into the individual's PPR form. Line of sight linkages and definition of improvement purposes are completed.

What is accomplished through the process just described is the translation of the organization's strategic plan into the individual's. Improvement pursuits for meeting customer needs with performance indicators (measurements) are identified but more importantly are able to be systematically addressed. The individual is now able to link what is done (job tasks), how tasks are done (processes), and how well the process works using measurements. Processes at the lowest level are connected to higher-level processes, first within the functional area, then cross-functionally. The total system becomes apparent and with it the individual's relationship to meeting the organization's mission, vision, goals, and objectives.

The line of sight process ties everything the organization does together. It is a tool for management in its leadership, management, and support of the organization. It is a tool for all employees in their understanding of what they do, its relationship to other activities, and what is important. It identifies the improvement objectives necessary to obtain the organization's goals. It provides a way for all to stay focused on the right things. It reduces waste. It provides a way for decisions to be based on fact rather than opinion. It combines philosophical intent and functional practice. It improves communication.

21 Management in a Quality Environment (Summary)

The art of management in a quality environment as well as those who practice it bears little resemblance to what is found in the traditional organization. Like quality itself, those who lead, manage, and support its implementation will find progress occurs slowly. This is the way of improvement, whether of processes or of individuals.

The previous chapter ended with the word *communication*, and that is the word that describes what this summary chapter and this book are most about. Though I use it as a noun, its substance is best understood in Webster's definition of the word as a verb: "transmit; make known; convey; share."[1] This is what management in a quality environment does. What is required of us and some of the ways to do it is what these chapters have shared.

Management cannot communicate, lead, manage, and support without doing what has been described. Certainly management can exist and go through managerial motions within the framework of the traditional organization. Management can follow past processes, policies, and practices; but, as I've illustrated, the traditional way is not the quality way.

The ingredients for a quality environment have been stated. It is customer focused and uses a customer satisfaction process. In it there is commitment and discipline. There is teamwork. Management and employee work together. There is a system for improvement. Changes from collective efforts evolve over time.

Quality requires a different type of management. It requires individuals who have the skills to lead, manage, and support. It requires management's attention to the environment, the culture, it creates and maintains. The job description for management in a quality environment requires competence in much more than functional task accomplishment. Management in a quality environment understands there is a system for doing what it is required to do.

Management in a quality environment understands there are managerial processes as well as operational processes. It is understood that these must complement each other to achieve and exceed customer needs and expectations. There is attention given to infrastructural processes, such as planning, budgeting, and individual performance appraisal, that not only support the environment but convey directly and indirectly as well what the organization is about.

Continual improvement in products, services, outputs, systems, and processes is sought. Management must cause change to be encouraged, not feared. Policies and practices must be consistent with and support the quality initiative. They frame the organization's attitude; they are another of management's messages of intent.

There are many responsibilities of management in a quality environment, many more than found in the traditional organization. None of these are more important than that of teaching and developing those who report to us. In a tactical sense, fulfilling this responsibility is the way improvement of individual tasks occur. In a strategic sense, it is the way the organization improves over time. Even here, the fundamental challenge is about how well we communicate.

The quality environment thrives on information, but even in this there is always challenge for management. People seem to thirst for information, so it often seems to employees there is not enough, or it is provided too slowly. Part of the challenge is in building employee trust.

It takes a long time to overcome the years of information hoarding of the traditional organization.

The quality journey is long and difficult. Only the most skillful and the most committed successfully reach its realization. Progress takes time, so patience is required. From the beginning management must understand and accept that continual improvement occurs a step at a time. It evolves. Years into the effort, one can look back and see how far the organization has come; how much has been achieved. Yet, in looking ahead, there will be more to do and more opportunity for further improvement.

The requirements of management are both singular and collective. They are about management as individuals and as a team. They are about the CEO, the line supervisor, and all of management in between. Quality is dependent on responsible individuals delving deep within themselves to change personal attitudes and practices. It is dependent on these same individuals joining with others to change organizational attitudes and practices. It is dependent on collaboration, not competition.

All of these requirements, these organizational needs and opportunities, are dependent on how management performs. There is no comparison between management in a quality environment and that of a traditional one. The true managerial professionals are those of quality. They are the ones who have mastered the complexities of leadership, management, and support.

Note

1. *Webster's New World Dictionary of the American Language, Second College Edition* (New York: The World Publishing Company, 1970), 287.

Appendix A

Memorandum

From: M. J. Richcreek   To: D. L. Lindemann   Date: 10/22/91
                            Vice Presidents
                            Department Heads
                            Assistant Department Heads

Re: Policy for Nonbargaining Unit Employees Displaced Due to
    Changes in Manning Needs or Reorganization

POLICY FOR EMPLOYEES WHO ARE DISPLACED DUE TO
CHANGES IN MANNING NEEDS OR REORGANIZATION

It is our intent to make changes in organization and reduction in manning levels as easy as possible on affected employees. It is also our intent
to keep employees within the Utility if other jobs become available that
they have the skills to perform. When outplacement is necessary, it is
our intent to provide a severance and outplacement package that will
assist the employee in finding comparable employment.

1. A department considering reorganization that will result in out-placement will first meet with human resources to develop a reorganization plan.

2. Department will develop a new organization or manning chart with job descriptions for remaining jobs in department. Employees will be notified of anticipated changes at least six months prior to manning adjustment.

3. Current employees will be interviewed for remaining jobs. Selections will be made on basis of best candidate for each position, not seniority. Candidates will be required to pass any applicable tests.

4. Employees will be notified of new staffing. Employees not offered permanent jobs will be given a six-month adjustment period, beginning at the time of notification, to find other employment within the Utility.

5. During the six-month adjustment period surplus employees will continue working in their regular assignment if possible. In those cases where the department does not have work the surplus employees will be assigned to a staff pool, managed by human resources, for the adjustment period.

6. The area making staff reductions will pay the salary and benefits of the employee while they are in the staff work pool.

7. Human resources will assign pool employees to temporary assignments based on their current job skills, to provide them with the opportunity to gain new skills and to expose them to other departments within the Utility. Assignments will be made based on needs in other departments.

8. At the beginning of the adjustment period, employees in the pool will receive a skills-assessment and career counseling seminar.

9. During the six-month adjustment period, employees will be encouraged to bid on other jobs within the Utility. If they bid successfully, they will be released to the new job immediately. If the new job is at a lower pay grade than their current job, they

will receive a one-time lump sum payment for the difference in their current pay and their new salary level. This amount will be based on the difference for 24 months. The new salary level will be in effect as soon as they report to their new assignment.

10. If they have not successfully bid on another job in the Utility at the end of the six-month adjustment period, they will be provided with severance payment of one week's pay for each year of service and three months of outplacement counseling.

Appendix B

Customer Satisfaction Process Guide: Assess Needs

Activity	Questions to consider	Techniques/tools to use
Identify customers, outputs	Who are the customers? What do you provide?	Storyboarding
List them all—there is no right or wrong answer!		
Select customer(s) or output(s) to focus on	What criteria should be used? Who are the key customers? What are the key outputs? Do you have different types of customers? Have you discussed the results of this step with your team advisor?	Pareto analysis Voting with dots What /how matrix Charts
If you are just starting, pick one—save the tough ones for later.		

Activity	Questions to consider	Techniques/ tools to use
Identify customer requirements Start with what you think is the customers' need, then ask them.	Do you *really* know what your customers want? Are there other needs that customers have not stated? Have you negotiated the requirements with your customers? Have you reviewed current and past data? Do your customers all have the same needs?	Surveys Focus groups Face-to-face meetings Industry data Interviews Internal consultants Suggestion box
Compare requirements (whats) and outputs (hows) Organize the data and do some analysis.	Are there needs with no outputs? Outputs with no needs? Are there specifications or measure for the requirements? How do your customers feel you are doing? How do your customers rate you against the competition? How do you feel you are doing?	Six steps What/how matrix Benchmarking
Analyze work process Make sure you get into the details!	How do you produce the output? Can you diagram it? Are there other ways to do the job? Do others do it the same way? Differently? Can it be simplified? How do you know if you are doing a good job?	Flowchart Fishbone diagram Check sheets Benchmarking

Activity	Questions to consider	Techniques/ tools to use
Identify process capability and performance	What is the process capable of providing? How consistent is the process? Can you always predict the results of the work?	Run charts and graphs Six steps
You may need more *data for this.*		
Determine output to provide	Does the output meet customer requirements? If not, why? Have you discussed your results with your team advisor?	Cost-benefit analysis Six steps
Test a few ideas— maybe the first idea isn't best.		
Produce outputs/ make changes	If changes are needed, do you have a plan outlining how you will get them done (who, what, and when)? Do you have everyone involved who needs to know about the changes?	Implementa- tion plan
Consider a pilot program or trial run		

Activity	Questions to consider	Techniques/ tools to use
Monitor process/ outputs Identify key success factors ___ Get enough data to give a clear picture	How to you measure performance? Where is improvement needed? What does the team advisor think? What should you monitor to guarantee that your product or service will continue to meet the needs of the customer?	Charts, graphs Benchmarking material Measures Fishbone diagram
Identify competitors or best-in-class ___ Brainstorm possibilities *then* narrow down.	Who is the best in marketing, financial, cost, quality, and delivery?	Research, interviews Storyboarding
Gather and analyze data ___ Get into more detail—reexamine cause-and-effect relationships.	Can you improve the process or output? What have you learned from your competitors or others with similar processes?	Benchmarking material

Activity	Questions to consider	Techniques/ tools to use
Develop improvement strategy Plan your work before working your plan!	What is your improvement target? When and how do you plan to do it? What help or resources will you need? What are the action steps and timetable? Are you continuing to monitor the process?	Six steps Strategy work sheet
Continue the process What do you want to work on next?	What is the next priority? Should you go into more detail on the same issue? Should you pick other processes or outputs?	Pareto analysis (see assess needs) Results of research and interviews

Suggested Reading

Fulfilling the opportunities available to management in a quality environment requires understanding organizational and managerial concepts, techniques, and philosophies fundamental to customer satisfaction. Beyond the basics, however, one must accept the fact that our learning is never done if we are to remain able to lead our organizations.

Albrecht, Karl, and Ron Zemke. *Service America!* Homewood, Ill.: Dow-Jones-Irwin, 1985.

Blanchard, Kenneth, and Spencer Johnson. *The One Minute Manager.* New York: Morrow, 1981.

Blanchard, Kenneth, and Robert Lorber. *Putting the One Minute Manager to Work.* New York: Morrow, 1985.

Blanchard, Kenneth, Patricia Zigarmi, and Drea Zigarmi. *Leadership and The One Minute Manager.* New York: Morrow, 1985.

Campbell, David. *If I'm In Charge Here Why Is Everybody Laughing?* Greensboro, N.C.: Center for Creative Leadership, 1980.

Carlzon, Jan. *Moments of Truth.* Cambridge, Mass.: Ballenger, 1987.

Collins, Brendan, and Ernest Huge. *Management by Policy.* Milwaukee, Wis.: ASQC Quality Press, 1993.

Covey, Stephen R. *The 7 Habits of Highly Effective People: Powerful Lessons in Personal Change.* New York: Simon and Schuster, 1990.

———. *Principle-Centered Leadership.* New York: Simon and Schuster, 1992.

Crosby, Philip B. *Quality Is Free.* New York: McGraw-Hill, 1979.

Deming, W. Edwards. *Out of the Crisis.* Cambridge, Mass.: Massachusetts Institute of Technology, Center for Advanced Engineering Study, 1982.

Harrington, H. James. *The Improvement Process: How America's Leading Companies Improve Quality.* New York: McGraw-Hill, Milwaukee, Wis.: ASQC Quality Press, 1987.

Peters, Thomas J. *Thriving on Chaos: Handbook for a Management Revolution.* New York: Alfred A. Knopf, 1987.

Peters, Thomas J., and Robert H. Waterman, Jr. *In Search of Excellence: Lessons from America's Best Run Companies.* New York: Harper and Row, 1982.

Peters, Thomas J., and Nancy Austin. *A Passion for Excellence: The Leadership Difference.* New York: Random House, 1985.

Senge, Peter M. *The Fifth Discipline: The Art and Practice of the Learning Organization.* New York: Doubleday, 1990.

Waterman, Robert H., Jr. *The Reward Factor: How the Best Get and Keep the Competitive Edge.* Toronto: Bantam Books, 1987.

Wheatley, Margaret J. *Leadership and the New Science: Learning About Organization from an Orderly Universe.* San Francisco: Berrett-Koehler, 1992.

Index

Advisors, assigning, 84–85
Assessment phase in customer
    satisfaction, 22, 23, 27–28,
    29, 181–85
Assimilation, 72
Attendance, 149
Autry, James, 38

Base compensation,
    157–58
Blanchard, Kenneth, 117–19,
    148
Budgeting, 90–91
    cross-functional review in,
        140–41
    establishing parameters in,
        94–95
Business process analysis,
    168–69

Change in process improvement,
    36
Citizens Gas and Coke Utility,
    x, 15
    activity description for,
        executive support team,
        67–68
    importance of employees,
        104
    mission, vision, and values,
        74
    quality curriculum at, 76–77
    quality process at, 42
    strategic planning at, 57,
        89–90
    teamwork at, 41–46
Collaboration, 5, 8, 14, 124, 164
Commitment, 49, 75
    definition of, 37

managerial responsibility for,
37–38
in quality environment, 35–39
Communication, 75, 76–77, 173
Compensation system, 153–60
Constancy of purpose, management responsibility for, 72
Continual improvement, 123,
162, 164, 174
Cost improvement, 6
Cost reduction, 4
Cross-functional budget review,
140–41
Cross-functional goals/objectives,
developing/revising, 136–37
Cross-functional performance
management team, 56–57,
83–84, 145–46
Culture, consideration of, as
soft issue, 15
Customer, defining, 12
Customer data, analyzing, 136
Customer focus, 101
evolution of, 48–49
management in, 56, 68–69
in quality environment,
11–19, 123–24
Customer needs assessment,
24–25
Customer satisfaction
coordinating and facilitating,
109–13
management in, 68–69
as methodology in quality
environment, 21–33
pursuit of, 19

Customer satisfaction process
(CSP), 26–27, 101–3,
126–27, 143–44, 168
assessment phase, 22, 23,
27–28, 29, 181–85
delivery phase, 22, 23, 28,
30–31
monitoring phase, 22, 23,
31–33, 85–86

Delivery phase in customer
satisfaction, 22, 23, 28,
30–31
Deming, W. Edwards, xii, 72,
169
Discipline, 49, 75
definition of, 39–40
in quality environment, 39–40
Displacement policy, 163–64,
166, 177–79

Education and training, 76
Employee appraisal system,
replacement of, by performance plan and review
process, 104
Employee empowerment, 4, 7–8
Employee involvement, 7
Employee needs/human
resource issues, 58
Employees, treatment of, as
customers, 25–26
Executive support team,
activity description for,
67–68
Expectations, 77

Fishbone analysis, 87
Flowcharting, 87

Gamesmanship, 90
Goals, management definition
    of, 92

Human resource management,
    teach/coach/mentor/
    develop in, 115–21
Human resource utilization
    changes in attitudes and
        practices about, 57–58
    system for, 125

Incentive pay, 157, 158
Incentive plan, 154
Internal customer, and evolution
    of management system, 66
*International Quality Study Best
    Practices Report*, 43, 48
Issue consideration, 84
Issue resolution, steps in,
    22, 24

Job evaluation process, 158
Job insecurity, 162
Juran, J. M., xii

Lateral opportunities, 165
Leadership
    in quality environment, 71–79
    styles of, 117–18
Line of sight process, 167–71
Line of sight team (LOST), 167
Listening, 77

Management
    commitment of, 35–39
    critical role of, 14
    customer focus in, 56
    in defining goals and objec-
        tives, 92–93
    definition of, 66
    in establishing budgeting
        parameters, 94–95
    job requirements of,
        124–25
    in pursuit of customer
        satisfaction and
        improvement, 109–13
    in pursuit of quality, 3, 5
    in quality environment, 22,
        24, 55–60
    role of, in use of human
        resource, 121
    and support of the quality
        process, 81–88
    traditional practices in, 66,
        124–25
    view of, as system,
        65–69
Management-by-objectives
    approach (MBO),
    7, 169
Merit pay, 157, 158
Mission, 72
Monitoring phase in customer
    satisfaction, 22, 23, 31–33,
    85–86

Needs assessment, 22, 23, 27–28,
    29, 181–85

Objectives, management
  definition of, 92–93
Organizational communication,
  126
Organizational teamwork, 126

Pareto analysis, 87
Partial enlightenment,
  4–5
Performance indicators, 78,
  93–94
Performance management team,
  cross-functional, 56–57,
  83–84, 145–46
Performance plan and review
  process (PPR), 59, 104,
  119, 143–52, 168
Planning
  mechanics of, 132–33
  role of management in,
  95–97
Planning and resource allocation
  process, 59–60, 126–27,
  131–41, 168
  coordinating and facilitating,
  89–97
Policy, developing and
  implementing,
  99–107
Preliminary resource needs,
  establishing, 139
Priorities, 77
  establishing in the traditional
  organization, 94
Problem solving, 6
Process, definition of, 68

Process improvement, 6, 162
  challenge of effecting, 15
  viewing employees as internal
  customers in, 26
Process optimization, 116–17
Productivity improvement,
  4–5
Profound knowledge, 169

Quality, 3
  challenges faced in implementing, xi–xii
  claims in pursing, 3
  definition of, 12
  implementation of, 36–37
Quality curriculum, evolution
  of, 50, 52
Quality environment, 41
  commitment in, 35–39
  creating and maintaining,
  71–79
  customer focus in, 11–19,
  123–24
  customer satisfaction
  methodology in, 21–33
  discipline in, 39–40
  evolution of, 47–52
  management needs in, 55–60
  management structure for
  new, 18
  management structure
  for traditional, 16
  teamwork in, 41–46
Quality focus, 71–72
Quality policies and practices,
  161–66

Recognition, 78–79
Report distribution listing, 87
Requirement elements, 83
Resource allocation process,
    role of management in,
    95–97
Resource needs analysis, 140
Results-driven focus, 7
Results orientation, 78

Safety, 149
Self-directed work teams, 7–8
Situational leadership, 117, 119,
    148
Skills improvement training,
    163–64
Statistical process control
    (SPC), 87
Storyboarding, 87
Strategic plan, terminology
    for, 90
Strategies, prioritizing,
    139–40
Strategy development, 137–39
Succession planning, 106–7, 127,
    165–66

Support
    management function in,
        81–88
    synonyms for, 81–82
System, definition of, 65

Teach/coach/mentor/develop,
    115–21
Team charters, reviewing and
    approving, 86
Team status report, analyzing,
    87
Teamwork, 5, 8
    definition of, 43–44
    in quality environment,
        41–46
Total quality management
    (TQM), 8–9, 73
Trust and respect, 77

Values, 72
Vision, 72

White, B. Joseph, 11–12
"Why?" factor in quality pursuit,
    49–50, 52